The Divine Power in Darkness

Green Witchcraft II reveals many techniques for working constructively with the dark aspects of the Divine. How can you use the dark as a positive force? Here are two possibilities . . .

> Dark energies are strong during the solar eclipse. *Green Witchcraft II* explains how to connect with the energies at this time to honor ancestors, visit with the spirits of the departed, charge magical tools, clear away anger and hostility, and even to overcome your fear of death—so that when the Sun reappears, the light will shine within you as well as upon the Earth . . .

> The lunar eclipse can convey you between worlds and help you find a companion from the Otherworld. Working magic at this time draws upon the power of the Goddess as the transformer, who can change your visions into reality. Perform a ritual to tap this power as the Moon passes into darkness (the Crone gathers your wish) ... as an emerging sliver of light appears (the Crone passes your wish into the arms of the Maiden) ... and as the Moon is revealed once more (the Mother gives birth to your desire) . . .

Green Witchcraft II describes many other ways you can connect with dark energies to release deep-seated fears and blocked emotions, achieve your goals, enhance your spiritual and magical practice, and align with the cosmic balance of the universe.

About the Author

Ann Moura (Aoumiel) has been a solitary practitioner of Green Witchcraft for over thirty-five years. She derived her Craft name, Aoumiel, to reflect her personal view of the balance of the male and female aspects of the Divine. Her mother and grandmother were Craftwise Brazilians of Celtic-Iberian descent who, while operating within a general framework of Catholicism, passed along a heritage of folk magic and Craft concepts that involved spiritism, ancient Celtic deities, herbal spells, Green magic, reincarnation belief, and rules for using "the power."

The Craft was approached casually in her childhood, being experienced or used as situations arose. With the concepts of candle spells, herbal relationships to magic, spiritism, reincarnation, Rules of Conduct, and calling upon the Elementals and the Divine already established through her mother's teachings in particular, she was ready to proceed in her own direction with the Craft by the time she was fifteen. In her practice of the Craft today, Aoumiel has moved away from the Christianized associations used by her mother and grandmother. She is focused on the basic Green level of Witchcraft and is teaching the next generation in her family. She took both her Bachelor of Arts and Master of Arts degrees in history. She is married, has a daughter and a son, and is a certified history teacher at the high school level.

To Write to the Author

If you wish to contact the author or would like more information about this book, please write to the author in care of Llewellyn Worldwide and we will forward your request. Both the author and publisher appreciate hearing from you and learning of your enjoyment of this book. Llewellyn Worldwide cannot guarantee that every letter written to the author will be answered, but all will be forwarded. Please write to:

Ann Moura (Aoumiel)
% Llewellyn Worldwide
P.O. Box 64383, Dept. K689-0
St. Paul, MN 55164-0383, U.S.A.
Please include a self-addressed, stamped envelope with your letter.
If outside the U.S.A., enclose international postal coupons.

GREEN WITCHCRAFT II

BALANCING LIGHT & SHADOW

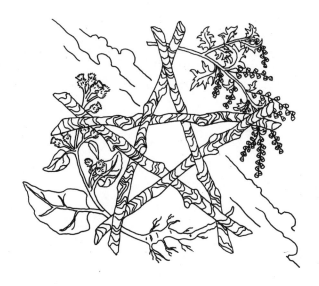

ANN MOURA
(AOUMIEL)

1999
Llewellyn Publications
St. Paul, Minnesota 55164-0383, U.S.A.

FIRST EDITION
First Printing, 1999

Cover design by Lisa Novak
Cover photo from Digital Stock
Interior illustrations by Carrie Westfall
Editing and design by Connie Hill
Based on original interior design by Rebecca Zins

Library of Congress Cataloging-in-Publication Data
Moura, Ann
    Green witchcraft II: balancing light and shadow / Ann Moura
    (Aoumiel) — 1st ed.
        p.   cm. —
    Includes bibliographical references (p.   ) and index.
    ISBN 1–56718–689–0 (pbk)
        1. Witchcraft.   2. Herbs—Miscellanea.   3. Magic.   4. Ann Moura
(Aoumiel)   I. Title.
BF1572.P43A58   1999
133.4'3—dc21   99-00000
                                                                    CIP

Llewellyn Publications
A Division of Llewellyn Worldwide, Ltd.
P.O. Box 64383, Dept. K689–0
St. Paul, Minnesota 55164-0383, U.S.A.

Printed in the United States of America

*This book is dedicated to the Elementals
and to the dark aspects of the Goddess and the God.
With our kith and kin, and with the dark
and the light are we made whole.*

Other Books by Ann Moura

Dancing Shadows: The Roots of Western Religious Beliefs (as Aoumiel)
Green Witchcraft: Folk Magic, Fairy Lore & Herb Craft

Contents

Publisher's Note

Certain herbs listed in the correspondences beginning on page 134 are considered unsafe for human consumption and/or handling. They have been included in this information as a cultural and historical reference, only. Substitute herbs are suggested for use in place of those that may be toxic. These herbal usages are not recommended as a substitute for traditional medical care. The publisher assumes no responsibility for injuries occurring as a result of such use.

1

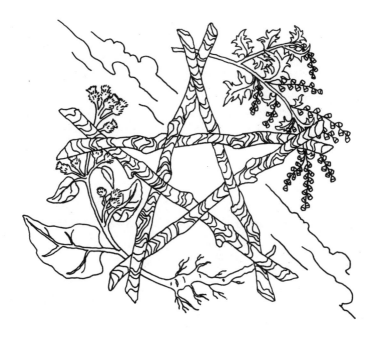

What Is Green Witchcraft?

The Green Craft is what I learned from my mother, and she from her mother. Beyond that, I have no record. Green Witchcraft is an herbal, practical, self-empowerment type of Craft that has three basic approaches. I know it as the Old Religion as it has passed through the Celtic-Iberian generations of my maternal line. It is the basic magical tradition that forms the foundation of a variety of pagan and witchcraft practices. "Green" comes from the use of herbs, the connection with Nature, and the lore of Greenwood, or the Wildwood.

The Green Witch is a natural witch, a hereditary witch, a kitchen witch, a cottage witch, a hedge witch, and generally, a solitary witch. This witch does not fear nature and the woods, but finds both comforting and homey. The Green Witch has a sense of belonging and

connection with the earth and the universe. This is what I attempted to share in my earlier book *Green Witchcraft* (St. Paul: Llewellyn
Publications, 1996).

My focus in this book is to expand that connection to include the
dark aspect of magic: understanding what that is, identifying other
tools and correspondences that relate to the Craft and to the dark
powers, and learning how to work with those powers. By learning
both the light and the dark sides of magical practice, a person functions as a whole being, connected to the whole of nature and
the universe.

The rituals of Green Witchcraft may be carefully planned and
conducted or they may be spontaneous and natural. The items recommended for use in spell work are natural, and imbued with the
essences and powers of the life-force within. The Green Witch
respects the powers and spirits of nature, and in working with them
knows that these are energies that never die, but may be directed to
accomplish a goal. Thus, when using an herb for a spell purpose,
the energy of that herb is addressed and invoked to work with you
in creating the effect you desire. When you burn the herb in a candle during a ritual, you are releasing that energy to blend with your
own for directing it in your magics. That energy, once focused on a
goal, is then sent to work the magic. Magic is, after all, the art of
creating changes.

With magics utilizing the dark powers, herbs and tools with dark
aspect energies are used to draw upon and focus the dark energies to
obtain a goal. This is not satanic or evil. There is no devil in the
Craft; evil lies in human intent. The dark powers are very strong and
can have a wondrous effect when directed to healing, for example.
Most important, however, is that until a person can accept that the
whole of nature, the universe, and life is a blending of light and dark,
a person is not totally connected to the All and is not a complete
witch. You must be able to recognize, use, and direct the power in all
its forms to be whole. A crash course in the Green Craft will help
get you grounded.

Green Practice as Folk Art

There are three basic approaches to the Green Craft. The first is under the umbrella of a mainstream religion, whether it be a Christian denomination or sects of Judaism, Islam, Buddhism, or Hinduism. The first three religions mentioned predominate in America and have in common the idea of their own variety of faith being *true*. This "True Faith" concept exists to some degree also in Hinduism, particularly in relation to its offshoot, Buddhism. In earlier Middle Eastern and European paganism, the religions of other pagans were normally treated as equal. Because the modern True Faith religions developed in pagan societies, each of these mainstream religions has retained its own natural, local magic tradition. These magics lie beneath the surface of the practiced religion and are either tolerated as superstition, shrugged off, or declared a heresy when a practitioner of the faith is discovered conducting them.

One way of practicing the Craft is to work magics using the new names of the deities of power. Each of the above-cited modern religions (being only 2,000 to 2,600 years old, except for Hinduism, which, while 3,000 years old, is integrated with India's 30,000 year old Dravidic tradition) has adopted some portion of the pre-existing pagan tradition into their own religious system. Many of these traditions are simply re-named to imply that the ancient pagan practice is actually a modern one. Some familiar things that have been adopted and accepted by the new religion of Christianity are Christmas trees, Santa Claus, the Easter Bunny, Easter baskets, Maypole dances, and Thanksgiving feasts. These were all pagan expressions of religious celebrations, and some of these (such as the use of holly, mistletoe, and Christmas trees) were vocally condemned by clergy until only a few decades ago (even President Teddy Roosevelt was against decorated trees). When you engage in these activities, you are recalling an older pagan heritage.

By the same token, the deities of a mainstream religion are easily assimilated into pagan culture. Thus you may identify the God as Jesus, Krishna, or whoever your culture calls divine, and connect with the symbolic power of that deity. With the Goddess, there is always a feminine power to call on: Mary, the Mother of God; Sarah; Hagar; Durga; the Mother of Buddha; or a female saint. Catholicism is famous for the use of saints in spells that are smiled at or ignored by the Church. People are not condemned for turning a statue of St. Anthony to the wall until he responds to your need, or burying in your yard a statue of St. Benedict or St. Joseph until your house is sold.

Many pagan magics have filtered through modern religions. When you use these practices—lighting candles at shrines, laying flowers at wells, using hex signs (still popular today with the Pennsylvania Dutch), and so forth—you are practicing the Green Craft as part of a mainstream religion. If you avoid walking under a ladder, toss salt over your shoulder when something is spilled, turn around when a black cat crosses your path, or make the horns with your fingers when someone looks at you strangely, you are practicing the old magics. The ladder is avoided lest you place yourself beneath others who use you as a step up in their own lives. You toss salt over your left shoulder to ward off future poverty of the item that was spilt. You turn aside to avoid the path crossed by the black cat to prevent others from thwarting your positive energies (unless you are able to connect with black cats and use that same energy to enhance your energies by redirecting against opposition). You make the horns to deflect and return any negativity sent your way by someone. These are all magics used under the cloak of mainstream religions.

My grandmother was a renowned healer. She used herbs in her work, and also invoked *The Power*. No one called her a witch, but people knew she could do things to help them. She did not abuse her power, and she was a respected member of her predominantly Catholic society. Her magics were much more than the ordinary superstitions just mentioned. She walked a delicate line to avoid persecution, blending the Old Religion with the saints and the god and goddess images of Catholicism to direct her energy. Modern witches who invoke various Christianized views of the energies—angels, saints, and the Holy Spirit—are working within the mainstream framework. Adapting a socially acceptable non-mainstream religion into witchcraft—such as Native American, Tibetan, Buddhist, or

Hindu beliefs—may also work to deflect criticism or to relate Craft practices with what is more familiar in society.

Green Practices as Personal Magics

This kind of Green Craft is a natural witchcraft that ignores the trappings of religion altogether. This is the elevation of Mannuz [my mother pronounced this "Mahn-nú": The Human; the Runic symbol is Mannaz: The Self] to oneness with the universe. The personal power of the witch is enhanced and focused through natural objects to be directed for accomplishing a goal. Because the Self is part of the All, the All is part of the Self and may thus be drawn within the Self, focused, and directed toward an objective. The Self becomes united with the Divine. Early ceremonial magic was based on the idea of absorbing the All into the Self to make the magician "God." The drawback to the ceremonial approach is that it requires acceptance of the cosmology and divinity framed by mainstream religion, distancing the magical practice from the Old Religion.

To perform magics of personal power, you have to accept that you have that power, but the power you draw on is based on what you have. If you are full of rage, you will draw that power. If you are at peace, you will draw that power. If you are envious and jealous, your power is muted and Self-limited, but if you can learn to redirect those feelings, turning aside the envy and jealousy, for example, and instead focusing on being better at what you feel you are lacking, your power will be enhanced. Power is dissipated and diffused if your approach is to bounce off the power of a rival. To hate another person because that person has something you think you lack will only drain you of your power. That person, too, is part of the All. Success will come only if you work *for* your Self, not *against* another's Self.

In this type of practice, the objects of nature take on great significance. Here is when the witch begins to codify a table of correspondences for a useable Spellbook, or Book of Shadows. The witch judges the effectiveness of associations of herbs and other plants to various aims. The colors and their impressions on the spirit and mind of the witch become consistent, but adaptable according to need and availability. Nature items used for their inherent energies might be feathers, rocks, sticks, pebbles, crystals, minerals, or wind, water, fire, and earth.

The Elementals are addressed and the use of ritual in conscious spellwork is developed. Magical tools such as knives (the black-handled ritual knife called an athame, and a white or brown-handled working knife called a bolline), wands, crystal balls, and divining cards are accumulated and imbued with the power of the witch. Oils and incenses are categorized, a Spellbook or Book of Shadows becomes the witch's guide to development of a successful practice. Spontaneous divination sometimes comes as a surprise, but as the Self joins more and more with the All, becoming Mannuz, things start happening naturally. This is a very energizing, self-empower-ment type of practice in which religion plays no part. It is you and the unnamed All working together.

With personal magic, you are free to draw upon anything that strikes your fancy, for all things have a relationship that you can sense. If you decide to enhance spells with the old names of the deities, you might be surprised to discover that many are now the names of demons and devils. Astaroth, Ashtoreth, Asamodeus, Lucifer, and others are demons and devils who were originally gods and goddesses (feminine endings altered to masculine to hide the fact that females have celestial power). Yet there is no "worship" here.

Names of Power were used by ceremonialists of old to create a frenzy of energy through subconscious, intuitive sensing of the names. If there are some names that strike you as intriguing or use-ful, they will assume the power that you ascribe to them. Hence, one witch's Och (an Olympic Spirit) will not have the same sensation as another witch's Och, and neither matches the ceremonialist's Och.

Anything that is personally sensed by the witch in this type of practice is acceptable for use. The pentagram, sigils of the planets, Elementals, etc. take on the meanings sensed by the witch utilizing them, provided the witch has sufficient power and self-confidence to mold what is being used. Here again, power comes from within to be Mannuz; the Self as God can direct power in any way desired.

For someone beginning the practice of the Craft, I would recommend avoiding the ceremonial trappings unless you feel comfortable with them and sense your own power.

There are a number of books such as *The Black Arts*, by Richard Cavandish and *The Complete Book of Spells, Ceremonies & Magic* by Migene Gonzáles-Wippler (see Bibliography for publication details) that refer to names of power, Olympic Spirits, demons, devils, angels, and archangels. Some names are variations of the kabbalic (Medieval Jewish magic system adopted by European ceremonialists) names of god. Others are derivations of dimly remembered names from pagan days, and still others are simply made up. Today this last style of invocation is called speaking in tongues and is accepted in some Christian denominations as a means of connecting with the Divine. It works in witchcraft as well.

The key to successfully practicing magic through the personal power of the witch is to be honest with yourself and follow your instincts. One of the universally recognized keys to power was stated simply by Socrates: "Know thyself." A witch not only manipulates the energies of the universe, a witch grows within to affect that which lies without. Perfection of the Self is an ongoing task and a worthy lifetime pursuit. It is part of the Old Religion that demands the individual accept responsibility for his or her actions. The Rules of Conduct covered later in this chapter are guidelines for your success.

Green Practice as Religion

This aspect of the Green Craft identifies the Goddess and the God as a working partnership with the dedicated witch. This is when the witch deliberately confronts the Divine as the Goddess and the God and calls upon them for aid, for comfort, for love, for unity. There is a self-initiation as an introduction to the deities of the Craft, followed later (a year and a day or even longer) by a self-dedication for complete union with the Divine. The practice of witchcraft is conducted with special days of religious observance. The Sabbats and Esbats are honored, and there may be other days of religious significance for the Great Goddess and Great God, honoring their various aspects and manifestations. A pagan book of days or Magical Almanac will give you an idea of special days you may want to observe in your practice of the Craft.

With the Craft as religion, the witch directs much of the magic through personal images of the God and the Goddess. The powers of the universe are identified in Green Witchcraft as male and female in balance. This is a great aid in focusing power and raising energy because it is a recognizable association. There are a number of pantheons to choose from if you do not have one you can relate to your family heritage. Sometimes in adopting pantheons you may come up with something that is rather mixed, but when you study religion, you realize that those disparate forms have the same roots. The Druidic impression of all gods/goddesses being the same god/goddess is applicable. Only the names for divine aspects vary from culture to culture, but the archetypes remain the same. As such, They may also be addressed without names, simply as Lady and Lord, or the God and the Goddess.

It is with the practice of the Craft as religion that rituals for life passages (marriage, divorce, birthing, coming of age, dying) and the four to eight Sabbats are often added to the Spellbook or placed in a separate Book of Rituals. I use both a Spellbook and a Book of Rituals in my practice. By drafting your own rituals, you may borrow from others (I gave examples of various rituals in *Green Witchcraft*) or fashion what feels right for you. You will find that variations will come to you, and that is normal. Over the years, a witch will fine-tune her or his personal practice.

There are witches who will elevate one deity over another, showing preference for an aspect of the Goddess or the God, for example, but Green Witchcraft is grounded in balance and partnership. With the Divine, the Two are One. One aspect of the All may be addressed, but the other aspect is not ignored. This is part of wholeness. Not only must you be able to unite the light and the dark in your Self, you must join the inner male and the inner female to achieve your Self as Mannuz, as the Divine within.

These are styles of practice of Green Witchcraft, not levels or advancements. What one witch finds most rewarding, another might not. All three styles of magical useage generate power equally, as this is determined by the power developed within the practicing witch. What remains basic throughout, however, and crosses all styles of practice are the Rules of Conduct.

The Rules of Conduct

My mother repeated these rules over and over to me. Her mother had done the same for her, and these same rules are found in different forms in various coven traditions of Wicca. Here is what she said to me:

- To use the power you must feel it in your heart and know it in your mind
- Be careful what you do
- Be careful who you trust
- Do not use the power to hurt another because what is sent comes back
- Never use the power against someone who has the power, for you draw from the same well.

To use the power you must feel it in your heart and know it in your mind. The Green Craft is very internal. You do not have to dress in black and look "witchy" to be a witch, but you do have to *feel* the power within you, and perhaps you will be drawn to black clothing or some particular, distinctive appearance. Addressing the light and the dark aspects of the Divine helps a person to accept that there is individual, innate power available. Like most magical practice, in the Green Craft that all-encompassing sensation of knowing is what moves the magic to work. Believe in yourself to believe in your magical power. Once you have felt that sensation of being in union with the power, you will never forget it.

Be careful what you do. With this power comes the warning to examine your motives and the direction in which you want to move your power. Again, this relates to knowing yourself, but also to understanding that there is a wide range of approaches to a problem or desire. Sometimes what seems to be the easiest route to gain an objective is a shortcut with an actual power range of limited satisfactory results to none at all. Think through what you are doing and the possible consequences.

For example, if your husband (wife) is flirting (or worse) with another woman (man), decide first if you can overlook this flaw in him (her) and want to maintain your relationship with your spouse. If you determine that you can and do, then you must decide how to direct your power to remove the problem. If the other woman (man) seems to be the main cause, simply doing a love spell for her (him) to find someone else will work. If the problem is the spouse or yourself, that needs to be addressed in order for the interloper to go away.

Be careful who you trust. As a witch, trust is very important. You trust the Divine and The Power as they are part of you, but there are less-connected people or people with less power who may fear a powerful witch. Many witches (I would guess most) stay in the broom closet simply to avoid unpleasantness from their neighbors or associates. In a coven situation, there is always the danger of one of the members turning on the others, either from a desire for power or abandonment of the coven path. It has happened, and the consequences can be anything from annoying (pamphlets, letters, phone calls) to alarming (public confrontation). Nothing dampens a witch's enthusiasm for group efforts more than for the behavior of one of the members to become out of hand. If you do join a coven, try to find people who are of an equal level of power and who do not try to dominate or mold the coven to one person's ideas. If something does not feel right, listen to your intuition, and avoid what generates your discomfort.

You should also be careful not to let others drain your power from you. If you are generous by nature, there will be people who will draw upon your power to enhance their own. This is a very subtle matter that can result in petty jealousies and rivalries. The person who siphons power from another tends to want to prove that the power experienced is his/hers, and usually the only way to make a determination as to the effectiveness of that power is to toss it at the one it was drawn from. Of course, this simply does not work.

10

Do not use the power to hurt another because what is sent comes back. When you fashion your spells, consider matters from the perspective of others. A kind heart is necessary, even in the midst of anger. You know instinctively when something is wrong, so to engage the power to harm another is to emphasize an out-of-control aspect of your Self that drains you of your power and de-energizes you. The result is that since your Higher Self knows this is wrong, your Higher Self will reverse the direction of the energy back into yourself.

In terms of spiritual development, casting harmful spells at others will eventually catch up to you. The Green Witch does not engage in this kind of spitefulness. There are many ways of dealing with problems. Some of these problems are an aid to your own development, and how you respond may have a lasting effect on you—for you are the one who will remember over the years what you have done. When people speak of near-death experiences in which their entire lives pass before their eyes, the most notable thing some of them mention is that they remember all the bad things they have done. When they awaken to life they are changed, for now they realize how much the consequences of doing wrong are, and they want to make amends. We are Self-judged. The Green Witch strives for connection with the All, and for Self-mastery.

Never use the power against someone who has the power, for you draw from the same well. Even more so than avoiding harm to your own power, using the power against someone who has the power is guaranteed to bounce right back. My mother never said anything about a three-fold return, only an equal return. Interestingly, the medieval ceremonialist had a similar idea, not of a thrice-fold law of returns (as is commonly seen in Wicca today), but of what was sent returning *if the spell failed.* The implication is that the sender has to have the power, not the recipient. This is reminiscent of what my mother said about people who have the power drawing from the same well.

The practical consideration here is that witches are family; family in the traditional sense of special people bonded together with ties of blood and heritage. This is the clan expressed through the power. If you are a witch, then witches are your kinfolk, and you do not work against your kinfolk. The importance of kinship is strong in Celtic society and remains a vital influence in lands touched by the Celtic peoples. Most Wiccan covens retain this admonition in the words, "Merry meet, merry part, and merry meet again." A witch should feel secure in the company of other witches, and the rule abides.

Manners

Much may be written on the matter of manners, but I only want to cover what in Green Witchcraft is required for successful encounters in Otherworld. Part of working with the dark powers involves the *Sidhe* (pronounced "Shee"), also called Fairy Folk, Other People, and Fair Ones. One of the reasons the witch contacts these beings is to gain their help in the magic being worked. The primary rule for working with the Fair Ones is that you have to give a gift to receive a gift. By giving a gift as a Fairy offering, you engage the Other People *in a relationship*. What they will typically accept are simple gifts of milk, flowers, wine, liqueur, whiskey, beer, oats, wheat, or herbs.

The Fairy Folk are spirits of nature. They are the energies and auras of plants, rocks, and waters. The Sidhe, or Elves, are called the Other People, and may be considered a separate elder species of Earth, or Fairy Folk energies that move apart from natural objects. Some people believe the Sidhe are as the spirit energies of deceased people who have moved from the Summerland (a tranquil land of rest and revitalization prior to rebirth) into Otherworld (the Undying Land) with no desire for rebirth. A person may also, in the Sanskrit meaning of the word, become Sidhe (energized) by opening awareness and letting the energy flow (the connection between India and the Sidhe is explored in my book, *Dancing Shadows*, Llewellyn Publications, 1994). Dwelling with the Sidhe can be experienced through astral travel, by meditation, and by a melting of the barriers between the worlds (such as by invitation).

The purpose of offerings is to invite the Other People to visit or dwell nearby, where their influence can be joined to yours in familiar surroundings. Offerings are also made as a means of participation in

Fairy celebrations. You can use offerings to ask for Fairy aid in a spell or other Craft work, or to seek a Fairy blessing, but overall, the offerings are an expression of kinship. You are linking yourself to them and they to you. In the practice of the Green Craft, offerings are also used as a show of your appreciation for their help and for their beneficial presence.

My mother was quite explicit about how one expressed gratitude to the Other People. We could never say, "thank you" because she said that it was insulting to the Sidhe. It is considered dismissive. Not only does a blunt thank you terminate the relationship you have built with the Sidhe, it also severs the tie between the Fair Ones and the gift. It is rather rudely perfunctory.

Instead of saying "thank you," you need to be creative and sincere. Say how much you like the gift, describe what you like about it, and express your afffection for the givers. There are a number of old Fairy tales that speak of Fairy gifts vanishing when thanks are given, or of great good fortune coming to people who express appreciation in a conversational manner.

Never reject a Fairy gift. These are the little items and tokens that appear seemingly out of nowhere. You will feel a sensation about them that will let you know what they are. Sometimes the gifts are simple things like seed pods that make perfect little altar bowls or a shiny pebble that sparkles at you. At times the Fair Ones will give you a gift simply to reinforce the ties between you and them. I once let the garden go for a time, then took myself in hand and tidied up the place. That night a single feather was laid at my doorstep—a gift that showed their appreciation and reminded me that the condition of the garden was important to them. By retaining your child-like sense of wonder in nature, you can open the gateways between the worlds with greater ease.

Another matter of manners is the old adage that you must be a good friend to gain a good friend. In the case of the Fair Folk, do not use the broom herb in Sidhe rituals or Otherworld workings. The odor of Scotch Broom is offensive to the Other People. If you want to do a lot of Fairy magics, broom plants should not be used in your yard or around the house.

Straw is sometimes inhabited by the Fairy Folk, so always handle it with care. You can also call a Fairy into straw, then lay the straw inside the doorway to your house to guard the house in your absence, or to ward against interruption while you are conducting your magics. If you must burn straw, you need to first forewarn the inhabitants and have someplace for them to move to.

Do not use iron in tools and Craft workings involving the Fair Folk, although an invocation of Wayland Smith (a Fairy black-smith) is a notable exception to this rule. He may be called on for aid in acquiring your own tools. Tools of copper, tin, gold, silver, and almagamations are preferable to iron. Pottery is also accept-able, as are other natural substances such as seed pods for bowls, shells for dishes, and gourds for cups. There is much of Fairy in these natural items.

While there is a charming little rhyme that states, essentially, that the Fair Ones do not like to be called "Fairies" but would prefer to be called "Good Neighbor" to be one, I think it depends on how a person uses these historic and familiar terms. If the manner is demeaning, it would not matter what word is used, and the same applies for a term used in a respectful tone.

With these basics of the Green Craft in mind, we can now proceed to discover the God and Goddess of Witchcraft, and the Elementals.

The Sun is setting, casting long shadows over the land. The cave darkens. The Sun disappears completely, taking the last of the colors with it, and the stars come out in the evening sky. A cool breeze brings the sweet scents of the night to you. You are at peace.

— Meditation —

Circle Casting and Releasing Fears Before Working with the Dark Power

The purpose of this meditation is to help release fears you might have so that you will be able to work with the dark powers of the Divine. The dark aspects of the Goddess and the God are named the Crone and the Hunter (or Dark Lady and Dark Lord, Lady and Lord of Shadows, and so forth). Because of the modern association of the dark with evil rather than as the balance of light, you may have come to fear the dark aspects. By understanding the dark aspects of Divinity, you become psychologically unified with the whole of the universe and empowered. Drawing on the Crone/ Hunter energy as part of the life cycle and accessing this power can lead a person to freedom from fears of the unknown, of death, and of the dark, bringing a person more fully into union with the All. The following meditation is suggested to help open the line of communication between you and the dark powers through facing and releasing the fears and anxieties that may have been part of your life for many years.

After a warm, candlelit bath, scented with herbs (rosemary, basil, thyme, and valerian) tied in a muslin pouch, you may want to dress in a comfortable robe, in clothes that you reserve for use in magical ritual and activities, or whatever feels natural for you. Be in a place where you will not be disturbed, and have the light off. When the meditation is over, refocus with the everyday world by eating and drinking something or attending to some household chore. Background music is not necessary, although some people like soothing music that imitates earth sounds—water flowing, the sea with the cries of seabirds, wind in the forest, and so forth. Place the items you will use and the refreshments inside the area you intend to use for your circle.

Creating a circle as a sacred space adds a sense of comfort and repose in a meditation. The following format is typical in Green Witchcraft and calls upon the Elementals for aid. The four Elementals, who will be discussed in Chapter 3, may be called at this time with your awareness that they are the four essences of life: Earth, Air, Fire, and Water.

To cast a meditation circle, light an incense such as sandlewood or frankincense, and light a purple candle. These scents and colors are symbolic of spiritual development and purification. If working outdoors, with a wand, stick, or twig, walk around your meditation area drawing a ring on the ground around you. If indoors, do the same, but envision the ring being drawn on the floor. The circle may also be drawn by pointing a knife or the index finger of the "power hand" (the hand you favor). As the circle is drawn, envision the energy of the Earth coming up through your body and shooting out as a blue light from the tool or finger you are using to indicate the circumference of the magic sphere around you.

Walk counterclockwise to form the ring in which you will meditate, and start at the North. The motion is counterclockwise to emphasize that the meditation is dark aspected. The starting position is North to emphasize the realm of the Dark God and the Dark Goddess, which is also the realm of the Elemental Earth. As you create the Circle, say:

> *The circle is drawn as a* **Circle of Power** *around me, above me, and below me in a sphere that passes through all boundaries in all planes.*

If your style of Craft uses religious references, you may add:

> *Cast and consecrated to the Lady and the Lord* [or deity names] *and charged by the powers of the Ancient Ones!*

Once the circle is drawn, set down the tool and take up the incense, walk around the ring, and waft the incense smoke with your hand, a dark feather, leaves, or an herbal sprig, and say:

> *This circle is cleansed and purified by fragrance and smoke.*

Set the incense in a safe place to the South of the circle, seeing it as the fire and smoke of ritual burial and cremations.

With the candle, go to the North of the circle and say:

I welcome thee, Elemental Earth, to my circle. As I am of flesh and bone, we are kith and kin (closely related), *and I call upon you to watch over me, aid, and guide me in my travels.*

Move to the West and say:

I welcome thee, Elemental Water, to my circle. As I am of water and blood, we are kith and kin, and I call upon you to watch over me, aid, and guide me in my travels.

Move to the South and say:

I welcome thee, Elemental Fire, to my circle. As I am of heat and energy, we are kith and kin, and I call upon you to watch over me, aid, and guide me in my travels.

Move to the East and say:

I welcome thee, Elemental Air, to my circle. As I am of thought and breath, we are kith and kin, and I call upon you to watch over me, aid, and guide me in my travels.

Set the candle down at the North of the circle in a place safe from falling or being knocked over. The candle holder should be placed on something, such as a tile, to steady it and to prevent damage to the surface on which it sits (particularly if indoors and on a carpet). It is the Light that shines in the Land of Shadows, the Lamp that lights the path to wisdom.

Sit in the center of the circle, facing North. If using a straight chair, place your feet flat on the floor (not with legs crossed) and hands resting palms up, one inside the other, on your lap or palms down over your knees. You may want to sit in a comfortable position on the floor with hands similarly placed or palms down over your knees. Your back should be straight to allow for an unconstricted flow of energy to pass along your spine. Now you are ready to release the mundane awarenesses of everyday living and move into your inner Self.

Breathe deeply and exhale, repeat. Now begin a simple breathing exercise of inhaling for two counts and holding for one, releasing for two counts and holding for one, etc. It is normal for your mind to wander when first beginning such meditations, but with practice it becomes easier to switch off. When the conscious mind becomes still, you are ready to open the subconscious mind and access the universe, so do not be surprised if your surroundings seem to change. It may take a few tries to get past this stage if you let your conscious mind alert you to the change and startle your subconscious mind into retreat. Once the conscious mind is at ease, you will be able to continue.

Now you are ready to identify and dispel your fears so that you will be ready to make contact with the dark power. You can address feelings of unfocused tensions and anxieties in this atmosphere of safety. Substitute another place that feels secure to you if the hermit's cave used in this example is not to your liking. Otherwise, envision yourself in a small, circular cave with an arched entry that gives you a view of the outside.

The stony walls and ceiling form an alcove around you. The ground is covered with moss and leaves, and you are sitting on a soft bearskin rug. You are facing the opening to the cave and can see that you are in a secure place near the top of a mountain, at a vantage point that allows you to look out over the forest beneath the mountain. The Sun is setting, casting long shadows over the land. The cave darkens. The Sun disappears completely, taking the last of the colors with it, and the stars come out in the evening sky. A cool breeze brings the sweet scents of the night to you. You are at peace.

Now that the scene is fixed mentally, focus on a question: "What do I fear?" or some form of this inquiry. Images may appear—these could include varieties of deaths, frightening faces, and so forth. Let the images come and go, but with each one that appears, ask, "Why do I fear this?" and listen for the answer, knowing that you are safe from any image that appears to you. Then ask: "What are these fears?" and you may be surprised to learn that the frightening faces are only masks. Allow the images to be unmasked, and realize that once a fear is known and exposed, it no longer has power over you.

After you have faced your own fears and unmasked them, you may conclude the meditation by simply saying, "Begone!" The images fade away, often with a little laugh—fear is only a game, after all, that you had allowed yourself to take too seriously. Stars shine again in the sky, you smile, breathe in deeply the night air, and as you exhale, the tensions of fear dissipate. You take another breath, and inhale the sense of all being right in the world. You are back in your meditation place.

Take a drink of a dark beverage such as grape juice, blackberry wine, or other such dark liquid, and eat a bit of dark bread, cake, muffin, or cookie. Now is a good time to relax and reflect on what you have learned. It may take several such visits to your hermit cave to face and overcome your fears, but you have made a start at becoming whole.

Once you are relaxed and alert to the conscious world, you may open the circle. Take up the candle and walk around the ring, pausing at the four points to bid farewell to the Elementals. This time, begin at the East and move to the South, West, and North, saying at each point:

Farewell, Elemental Air! We have shared this circle in kinship. Go in peace, and my blessing take with you!

Then proceed to Elemental Fire, then Water, and finally, Earth.

At the North, after the Elemental Earth has been farewelled, pinch or snuff out the candle, and set it down. Then take up the wand (or whatever tool was used to draw the circle) and walk the circle from North to East to South to West and back to North (the opposite way you walked to draw it) with the tool pointed to the ring. Envision the blue light returning into the tool and passing back through you into the Earth, and say as you walk:

The circle is opened, yet remains a circle as the power flows in me and through me.

Touch the tool to the middle of your forehead to *seal* the energy at the point of your psychic center (called the Third Eye). Ground yourself to drain off excess energy by touching the Earth (floor) with the palms of your hands, and put away your tools.

By releasing your fears, you are able to embrace unity with the universe and all it contains, both light and dark. You may need to perform this meditation several times on different days in order to feel fully freed from the fears that have held you captive. The hermit cave is always there if you need to address a new fear. Your inner Self is in the process of becoming whole and unburdened, and when you expose your fears to scrutiny, you are empowering yourself so you will feel capable and worthy of oneness with all aspects of the Divine.

2

Who Are the Goddess
and the God?

Divine Power in Light

The term *goddess* applies to the feminine aspect of the Power, but even this is more a matter of how you feel about the divine feminine than how the feminine of the universe is. She can be addressed as the mother goddess of fertility and birth; as the lady of Fairie's Greenwood, the protectress of the wilderness and the animals; as the Moon goddess of emotions and intuition; as the Earth goddess of the harvest and the waters of life. Names may be applied to her in any of these forms, and many of the ancient names of the goddess overlap in meanings. Most of her sacred names translate into descriptions or are other language forms of the term "lady" or "goddess."

The *god* is the masculine aspect of the Power, and again, the term depends upon your own impressions of the divine masculine rather than how the masculine of the universe is. He can be addressed as Father, as the Horned God of fertility, animals, and wildlife; as the Greenman god of vegetation, woodlands and fields; as the Sun god of life and energy; as the Earth god of grain and harvests.

These are aspects of the goddess and the god as drawn from the Power in Light.

Then there is that wondrous figure of the Divine as seen in every ancient society and religion: the Divine Androgyne. Here at last is the true nature of the power—not feminine or masculine, but both or neither. It is the true *whole*, the unified universe, the power compleat. When you can grasp that sexuality is defined by the individual, then you can understand that the power transcends that definition, whatever that definition is. The power is expansive, and as personal or nonpersonal as the individual is willing to allow it to be.

This is the basis for so many different approaches to religious practice: sex as metaphor for the Divine; celibacy as metaphor for the transcendence of the Divine; oneness as metaphor for the personal Divine; and nirvana as metaphor for the nonpersonal Divine. Hence, there are deities that have characteristics of sexuality and fertility; deities of austerity; deities of caring; and deities of detached omnipotence. Various religions emphasize different aspects of the power and create their own mythology to explain and sustain that aspect in a society. When there are conflicting views over which aspect of the Divine power a community should focus on for the benefit and control of a societal unit, warfare often erupts.

To me, naming the Divine imposes limitations on them and how they relate to me and me to them. Once we understand that the mythologies of all the gods and goddesses are only stories meant to enhance our comprehension of the powers of the universe, those stories lose their importance. The powers themselves—direct and potent and drawn through the witch—are what matters. In a time of crisis, seeking the aid of a deity by a name and trying to envision the myth and sensation that identifies that deity can be a singularly empty investment.

Instead, facing the trials of real life by addressing the very real powers is how you draw the force and energy into yourself to direct it for your purpose. There comes a time in everyone's life when the myths and names no longer serve a purpose; when calling upon one name or another leaves you feeling hollow inside. This is when you know you have gone beyond mythology and names, and are ready to confront the power, one on one.

For others, the singular moment of crisis may be a time when the mythology helps in focusing the power, but more often than not, when religious people talk about such a time of testing, the emphasis is on how the faith is tested, how religion is lost, how the faith is lost. For those who have a fortuitous result and regain their faith, the impartial observer can see, instead, that the person involved in this time of testing drew upon an inner strength and successfully forged a connection with the power as yet unlabeled to that person.

Hence, the *signs* of divine intervention for one person of one religion will match those of another person of another religion. It is the manifestation of the power that is drawn, focused, and directed that is experienced first and foremost, and the identifying of that power with a known social mythology comes later.

So who are the Goddess and the God of the Craft? In Green Witchcraft, names are irrelevant. Until you face these powers directly, any name or no name may be used. The deities of the Craft bear the names of ancient gods and goddesses of human history, but even these names are meanings rather than proper nouns. They are nouns with capitalized letters to make them proper nouns. Just as when people name their children Sky, Dawn, Summer, and so forth, the name has its own separate meaning, which is now *applied* to a person who possesses an individual personality.

When you call upon the Divine by names, you are actually addressing a trait or characteristic of the power that you identify, usually through knowledge of the myth attached to that name. Sometimes, the name alone has an effect on you and the mythology is irrelevant. There are people who believe that the name alone is powerful and that if you call upon a name that someone else associates with negative energy, you will accidentally draw negative energy and counteract your purpose, but that is not how magic works in witchcraft.

Magic comes from within. How you pull energy into yourself, focus it, direct it, and release it is the conduct of magic. You literally conduct magic as energy to create change. You may need to shift through the power to find that essence you want to address and direct. Therefore, the lack of names for these energies is not a detriment to practicing the Craft—and conversely, any name used will work according to how you feel about it.

Divine Power in Darkness

There are also Dark Aspects of the same two divine feminine and masculine energies: the Crone goddess of wisdom, death, and passage and the Hunter god who initiates those aspects through the Crone. Again, the archetype rather than the name is what matters in the Green Craft. Although names and mythologies exist for the dark powers in all cultures, these may be limiting to the practitioner due to the mythologies that may no longer apply or that fail to impress an individual with the meaning intended. If there are names of dark powers that appeal to you, then these can be useful, but often the names alone convey an impression to the subconscious mind that is not matched in the mythologies as they have survived after centuries of repression, and thus can be useful.

Solar Eclipse

The solar eclipse is the symbol of the Dark Lord, also called the Lord of Shadows, the Leader of the Wild Hunt, Hades, Pluto, and the death and resurrection aspects of Cernunnos, Dionysus—and on a cosmic level, Shiva, among others. The Christian comparison is that portion of the crucifixion of Jesus when he descends into hell then resurrects. As such, the solar eclipse (the Bible story of the crucifixion states the sun darkened at 9:00 A.M.) is a time for ritual observances that link the practitioner with the death passage portion of the cycle of life.

This is an opportunity to connect with the Shadowlands or the Underworld and to face one's own fears and uncertainties about death. By confronting death through meditation, the face of Death is unmasked. The face one sees may initially be grotesque and horrible, but once the beholder accepts that this is also the face of the giver of life's energy, that face changes and is beautiful to behold. This is the significance of focusing on the passage. By facing our fears, we gain insight and freedom—death is no longer to be feared.

Once a person is no longer fearful of death or the Underworld, the solar eclipse becomes a good time to honor ancestors, visit with the spirits of the departed, charge Craft tools of dark power magics, and honor the Dark Powers.

The eclipse does not last very long, so lengthy ceremonies would not be in order unless you create one that begins prior to the eclipse and encompasses the eclipse. Instead, if you are feeling *connected*, you may simply want to light some incense and a candle and invite someone departed to visit with you just for a little while so you can ask for guidance, tell the person you love him/her, offer forgiveness or ask for it as the case may be, or use the time to celebrate your union with the Crone and Dark Lord. It is also a good time to end anger and hostility, so that when the Sun reappears the Light will shine within you as well as upon the Earth.

Lunar Eclipse

The lunar eclipse is the symbol of the Crone, also called Rhea, Hecate, Hel, Mother Hulda, the Snow Queen, Bone Mother, Demeter (when searching for Persephone and the earth's vegetation dies), and Sekhmet. It is significant that the eclipse does not relate to the Crone as Lady of Wisdom, who is part of the Crone image with the waning crescent-moon part of the lunar cycle, but focuses on the Lady as Passage. Now is a fine time for dark magics and Sidhe magics.

The Lady as Passage offers transit between the worlds to Otherworld and the Sidhe, and her moon is the best time for magics involving the Other People, or for seeking a companion from Otherworld. The following ritual combines these.

This lunar event additionally provides a person with the opportunity of drawing the subconscious into manifestation, which draws upon the power of the Goddess as Transformer. She is the Dark Lady of the subconscious, intuitive mind, Who then transforms the practitioner's innate desire/will into reality as She Herself changes into the Mother. She gives birth to your desire in a ritual or meditation performed at this time. You focus on what it is that you want to have and, as the Moon passes into darkness, envision that desire being gathered by the Crone, then passed into the arms of the Maiden as the sliver of Moon appears heralding the ending of the eclipse, and brought into manifestation by the Mother as the Moon is finally revealed.

Dark Aspect Meditations

Death of the individual has traditionally been brought about by the Dark Goddess in order for there to be a rebirth. This is the image of Demeter and Persephone, and it is the demonstration of the changing of the seasons. The significance of the death brought by the Dark Goddess lies in its promise—the renewal of life in a new form—for the death is not finite nor permanent, but a transition, and She is the One Who Transforms. The Crone is also the Maiden and the Mother. That the old pagan cosmology has relevancy in the face of modern science and understanding is an impressive statement for the enduring truth of the regeneration of energy in matter.

To regain a feel for the cycle of life with death as a transition into new life, create your circle and try a meditation that takes you riding with the Hunter as he gathers the souls of the dead with his Wild Hunt, called the Rade. You may want to record the following meditation first, then play it back. Here you can get a feel for how the Dark Lord and the Crone work together as one. Meditations are useful tools for self-improvement and creating a connection between the practitioner and the universe. You do not need to meditate to practice the Craft, but it is a lot easier to perform magic when you are in union with the Divine and the Elementals. The "Ride with the Rade" meditation was first published in *Llewellyn's 1998 Magickal Almanac*.

Meditations From Real Life Experiences

I have found that some of the most valuable guided meditations are based upon personal experiences, places visited, and memorable sights and sounds. To be effective, the person doing the meditation adds an individual focus and perception that opens new pathways from the basic one offered. I based the Crone meditation on my own experience when my mother died. I learned she was in the hospital and fading quickly, but it was an eight-hour drive to get to her. For six hours as I drove, I worried that she would pass on before I got to see her. At one place, underbrush was being burned for a widening of the highway, and the smoke rose in a huge pillar high into the sky. As I drove, my mind was on how much time it would take me to get to the hospital. I looked up at the billowing smoke, and the clouds seemed to instantaneously transform into the image of the Crone. She was heading for the town where my mother was, and she was a hideous, terrifying sight as she turned her head to look down at me.

In my mind I heard her voice say, "I am going for your mother, but I will wait for you."

The first impact of her words was the knowledge that my mother was indeed dying. The second was that I could rest assured I would be able to talk with her before her passing. At a time like this, the whole process of death and passage becomes personal and imminent. I trusted that the vision was authentic and the message was as I heard it. This is part of the "perfect love and perfect trust" so often discussed in the Craft.

My fear of the separation that death brings vanished. I put my trust in the Lady, and I whispered, "I am not afraid of you because I know that you are also the Mother."

I knew my mother would make the passage into the arms of one who loved her. In the moment I said those words, the image in the clouds changed dramatically into the most beautiful woman I had ever seen, smiling down at me. Her voice came into my mind, "Only those who do not know me fear me."

Lord of Shadows hidden within the Lady of Darkness, together they hold the darkness in Balance. He is the Passing, She is the Passage, together they move from life into life.

— Meditation —
Ride with the Wild Hunt*

Sit in a darkened room. Breathe deeply and exhale, repeat. Now begin a simple breathing exercise of inhaling for two counts and holding for one, releasing for two counts and holding for one, etc. This will help you to relax and clear your mind. Once your mind is calm, the noise of stray thoughts is vanquished, and you are in your quiet inner space; listen and hear the distant thundering of horses' hooves. A horn sounds far away, and the noise of riders seems to become more distinct. Now you hear the pounding of horses' hooves coming closer; the rattle and squeak of harness and saddles; the heavy breathing of the beasts; and again the blast of the horn; and you know it is the Wild Hunt approaching.

You call out: "May I ride with the Rade until break of day?" and the Hunter calls back to you: "Catch hold my hand and dare not let go!" and as He passes, you grasp the hand held down to you and are amazed at the fluid strength that quickly pulls you up to sit before the Hunter upon His mount. You hold fast to that hand and watch the Rade from your privileged seat.

Over mountaintops and through valleys; over seas and flood plains; past great cities and small villages you ride; and you become aware through the dark swirling clouds around you that shadows rise up from the lands you have passed and join the Wild Hunt in its headlong race through the dark. The Rade races before the sunrise and now you see that the land is more familiar. You recognize your own local countryside, towns and cities, and the Hunter says: "The dawning comes and you are back again from whence you sprang upon my steed. My bargain is kept—you rode with the Rade until break of day."

In an instant that strong arm and powerful hand has dropped you gently onto the ground. You see before you a great earthen mound with a carved stone gateway, and you are reminded of a pregnant woman's full belly, and yet the entrance is ancient. You see the Crone, gray and shriveled, dressed in tattered shrouds, standing in

---

* *Llewellyn's 1998 Magical Almanac*. Used with permission of the publisher.

31

the dim entry and she says: "You must pass through me to be born of me!" Now you realize how much the Wild Hunt has grown in size; with laughing riders and plunging horses, you watch as the Hunter leads the Rade through the entry into the Shadowland. The gateway vanishes; the dawn breaks; you breathe easier and are at peace. You can feel the warmth of the morning sun. The landscape fades and you return to normal consciousness.

By facing the entrance to the Underworld and the power of the dark aspect of the Divine, a person comes to understand that the dark is part of the necessary balance of life and not something to fear. The uniting of the dark and the light within the individual reflects the union of these two aspects in the flow of the universe, and that offers a person a sense of wholeness and peace.

— Meditation —
Unmasking the Crone

Meditations help people to face and overcome what they fear, so utilizing my own experience and vision, you may want to carry the previous meditation a step further to confront the Crone in her domain. This time as you are riding with the Hunter, approaching the place where you first called to him, ask him to let you remain a little longer.

Let me tarry awhile and see the great spiral.
Let me ride with thee now into thy dark bower.
Let me see the path followed and how the lives flow.
Let me ride with the Rade as you travel below.

The Hunter nods his antlered head and now you see the mound in the gray light of early dawn. Again, the Crone, in her tattered shrouds, stands before the entrance and you hear her cry out, "All must pass through me!" and you see her getting closer as the horses continue their wild plunge into the gateway.

There is a sudden roaring wind in your ears; a sound like spinning millstones grinding corn fills your consciousness; the darkness closes around you and you smell a scent that reminds you of the damp, dark, rich earth. The temptation is to close your eyes, but you force yourself to keep them open and realize that the shadow flying past your face has a substance like cobwebby shrouds and the cold dank air of deep caverns. You are passing through the Crone, and feel nauseous with the sensation of death, the noxious odors of disease and decay, and the scrabbling thin fingers scratching at your flesh.

Yet the horses ride on and the Hunter holds you firmly in his grasp, and you cling to him and call out to the fearful image of the Crone as you pass through her: "I know who you are! You are the Mother of All, and I do not fear you!"

She laughs and turns to you as you pass through her, and, incredibly, you see a lovely lady, smiling and more beautiful than words can describe, and you laugh with her. You hear her gentle voice as she replies to you, "Only those who do not know me fear me."

Suddenly, it is as though you had been a child all along, playing in a dark room, letting your imagination frighten yourself. Now you know that the face of the Crone hides the lovely Mother who awaits you with open arms, and you feel secure, loved, and at peace.

The Hunter races his mount through the dark realm, and you see spirits taking their rest by still, dark pools overhung with cypress branches and long gray moss. Soft, silky grass and delicate pathways beckon to you to walk and relax. You are tempted to stay here and enjoy the Shadowland with its night-blooming flowers and air scented with lilacs, but the Hunter does not let you down from his steed.

Through a dark forest padded with the sodden leaves of autumns past you now race, and then you burst upon a sunlit meadow. There are children playing and the shining bright Other People wave to you as you pass. Spirits appearing to be of all ages and ageless move in this bright place, and you realize that there is light and warmth here, for you are in the Summerland, close to the Otherworld of the Fair Folk. Still the Hunter holds you tight, and you sense rather than see that you are passing through another kind of veil.

"Here goes one who has rested and now desires to resume the great dance of life," the Hunter whispers in your ear and mind.

You look and see a shadowy figure as it appears to be moving through a grayish swirling mist towards a distant light, and you realize that this is a spirit departing the Shadowland to be reborn.

Now your own race is ending and you see the dark earth close in around you, pebbles and snails, and earthy creatures wriggle by on many tiny legs, or none at all. The ground seems to open and a starry night appears before your eyes, and when you look back around past the Hunter, you see the great mound behind you. He clasps you with one strong hand and effortlessly swings you off his mount and onto the ground, then laughing, rides off into the night, the Wild Hunt behind him on their rounds anew.

You see the dawn coming now, and as you return to normal awareness, you are at peace, and hold the memory of the beautiful lady who laughed with you when you penetrated her disguise. You know that life is eternal. There is no death, only passage.

— Dark Moon Ritual —
Consecration of a Dark Aspect Tool

Various tools may be dedicated during a Dark Moon for use in dark aspect rituals. A gourd with seeds inside is useful for shaking during meditations that take the practitioner into other worlds. It can also be used in dark-focused rituals for calling upon the Dark Lord and Dark Lady—the God and the Goddess in their aspects of chaos, death, transformation, and passage into new life. The gourd is shaken by the crook of the neck with one hand and patted against the palm of the opposite hand in a circular fashion. Other tools that may be consecrated during a Dark Moon are the black mirror, crystal ball, Tarot decks, stones, crystals, and even Familiars.

Here is a sample Green Witchcraft ritual for the Dark Moon that includes a ritual for consecrating a tool. A Craft Name is one others may know you by, but the Working Name is known only to the Witch and the Divine, so if you are working with a group use your Craft Name.

Candles are set at the Quarters (North, East, South, and West) and may all be purple, white, or black (place them so they will not get knocked over or melt onto carpeting or floor), or you may want to use four rocks, gems, or stones placed at the Quarters.

Light an incense that is not overly spicy or floral, although lilac is an exception as an evening scent (some pre-packaged scents include names like Night Lady), or burn mugwort herb.

Have the following items on the altar: three purple or black candles in a triple candelabra or in separate holders (right side for the God, left side for the Goddess, and center for both), incense and burner you can carry, matches, small bowl of water, small dish of salt (rock or sea salt), a pentacle (best if wooden or tile), a cup or goblet containing a dark fruit juice or blackberry wine (or elderberry wine, cassis liqueur, or Opal Nera, a liqueur of elder and anise), a small cauldron, a purple or black votive candle and holder, a piece of dark fruitcake, or other dark cake or bread, candle snuffer, anointing oil, knife (athame), wand, and tools to be dedicated.

Dark Moon Esbat (Beginning)

Sweep the circle deosil (N-E-S-W) with the besom (but *not* one made of broom or Scotch Broom if you work with an Otherworld companion; straw, grasses, or leaves are fine), and say:

> *As I sweep this circle, may it be cleansed and made ready for my work.*

Clap your hands three times, and say:

> *The circle is about to be cast and I freely stand within to greet my Lady and my Lord of Shadows.*

If using candles at the Quarters, light them by taking the center altar candle around the circle to each Quarter candle, moving deosil (clockwise: North-East-South-West), and saying:

> *I call upon the Light within Earth to illuminate and strengthen the circle* (envision the magma core, the molten center of the Earth).

> *I call upon the Light within Air to illuminate and strengthen the circle* (envision the aurora borealis, the

35

Northern Lights formed by the Earth's magnetic field, and seen as curtains of light in the night sky).

I call upon the Light within Fire to illuminate and strengthen the circle (envision the blue/white of flame).

I call upon the Light within Water to illuminate and strengthen the circle (envision the blue/white lights of bio-luminescent sea creatures at night).

If using stones at the Quarters, move around the circle in the same manner, but raise up the candle at each stone and use the same invocation (a different color/type of stone for each Quarter could be used to emphasize the essence of the represented Elemental).

Return to the altar, place the candle back in its holder, take up the knife, and say:

*I draw this circle in the presence of the Dark Goddess and the Dark God to be a place where they may manifest and bless their child,*_____ (Craft Name/ Working Name).

Walk around the circle widdershins (counter-clockwise: N-W-S-E) with the knife lowered, envision a blue light shooting from the tip to form the circle boundary, and say:

This is the boundary of the circle in which only love shall enter and leave.

Return to the altar and put the tip of the knife into the dish of salt and say:

Salt is purification, preservation, and life. I bless this salt to be used in the circle in the names of the Crone Goddess and the Dark God, _____ (names such as Hecate and Cernunnos, or simply use those terms).

Add three portions of salt to the water bowl (you are creating "holy water"), using either the tip of the knife or your fingers, and say:

> *Let the blessed salt purify this water for use in this*
> *circle. I consecrate and cleanse this water in the names*
> *of the Crone and Dark Lord, _____.*

Take the consecrated water bowl and sprinkle water from it around the circle, moving widdershins (N-W-S-E), and say:

> *I consecrate this circle in the names of the Crone and*
> *Dark Lord, _____. This circle is conjured a* **Circle of**
> **Power** *that is purified and sealed.*

Return the bowl to the altar, take up the censor and move around the circle widdershins to cense it, then return it to the altar.

Put a drop of anointing oil on your fingertip, make a Solar Cross on your forehead, then a Lunar Spiral over the Cross, and say:

> *I, _____, am consecrated in the names of the Dark*
> *Lady and Dark Lord, _____, in this their circle.*

Call the Quarters by taking the wand and addressing the Quarters of the circle where the candles or stones are, holding the wand aloft with arms open at each site, and saying at the appropriate Quarter (N-W-S-E):

> *I call upon you Elemental Earth* (Water; Fire; Air) *to*
> *attend this rite and guard this circle for as I have body*
> *and strength* (blood and feelings; fire of life; breath and
> thought), *we are kith and kin!*

For Elemental envisionings, you might see a wolf for Earth, an owl for Air, a phoenix for Fire, and a sea serpent for Water.

Return to the altar and use the wand to draw the symbol of infinity (the figure 8 laying on its side) in the air above the altar—this is the symbol of working between the worlds; set the wand down. Pick up the knife in both hands and raise it over your head and say:

> *Hail to the Elementals at the Four Quarters! Welcome*
> *Lady and Lord to this rite! I stand between the worlds*
> *with love and power all around!*

37

Next are the Libations of Greeting. Set down the knife, pick up the cup of wine (or liqueur) and pour some into the cauldron to honor the Divine with the first draught, then take a sip from the cup.

Raise the wand in greeting and say:

I, _____ , who am your child, stand between the worlds and call upon my Lady as Crone and my Lord as Shadow to hold communion with me. I affirm my joy of union with the Divine and acknowledge Your blessings upon me. What I send returns to me, and I conduct my Craft accordingly.

Set the water bowl on the pentacle, hold the knife over it, and say:

Great Lady, bless this creature of Water and of Earth to Your service. May I always remember the cauldron waters of rebirth and the many forms of being. Of Water and Earth am I.

Hold up the water bowl and say:

I honor You, Great Lady!

Replace the bowl on the altar, put the censer on the pentacle, hold the knife over it, and say:

Great Lord, bless this creature of Fire and Air to Your service. May I always remember the sacred fire that dances within all life and hear the voices of the Divine. Of Fire and Air am I.

Hold up the censer and say:

I honor You, Great Lord!

Return the censer to the altar and hold up the goblet and say:

Power and Grace; Beauty and Strength are in the Lady and the Lord. Patience and Love; Wisdom and Knowledge; you are Endings, Passages, and Beginnings. I honor you both!

Pour a second libation and take a second sip from the cup (a third and final libation, comes with the concluding Cakes and Wine, so be sure to start with enough).

Consecration of the Dark Aspect Tool

Using the knife, inscribe the tool with the magical symbols you have selected, and with your Craft Name in runes, ogham, or other such alphabet used in magical practice.

Consecrate the tool to the Elementals by sprinkling it with blessed water and passing it through the incense saying:

> *In the names of the Dark Lady and Dark Lord, _____ ,*
> *I consecrate this [name of item] to be used in my*
> *practice of the Craft. I charge this by the Elemental*
> *Earth and Elemental Water* (sprinkle with salted water)*;*
> *by the Elemental Fire and Elemental Air* (pass through
> the incense smoke)*. This tool is now by Elemental*
> *powers bound to aid me in my work. So mote it be!*

Set the tool on the pentacle and say:

> *Great Lady and Great Lord, together in the darkness of*
> *this Moon, veiled from my sight yet seen with my inner*
> *sight, you dwell within for you are endings and new*
> *beginnings, the death that leads to new life; you are the*
> *Promise and the Love Manifested. Let this tool be*
> *imbued with your power to aid me in my dark journeys.*

Light the votive candle from the center candle, and say:

> *Let this small light illuminate the dark path to the*
> *Realm of Shadows.*

Then pick up the tool with your right hand, hold it up, and with the left hand held so the palm is parallel to the ground, say:

> *Lord of Shadows hidden within the Lady of Darkness,*
> *together they hold the darkness in Balance. He is the*
> *Passing, She is the Passage, together they move from*
> *life into life. With my hand in theirs, I call upon them*

*to share their presence with me and pass dark power
into this* (tool) *that it may be sanctified to serve me in
my dark journeys.*

Envision the dark energy shooting up from the ground, into the palm of the left hand, traveling through the left arm, across the shoulders into the right arm, up the right arm into the right hand, and into the tool.

Set the tool on top of the pentacle and kneel so that both palms now rest on the ground and say:

*As what is sent returns, so I return to you the power so
graciously sent to me. My* (tool) *is sanctified through
Power and Grace, through flesh and blood, and made
ready for my use. So mote it be!*

Stand and remove the tool from the pentacle, but keep it on the altar; snuff the votive candle and say:

*The path is closed; darkness returns to the
Shadow Realm.*

If no consecration of a tool is involved, simply leave out the parts involving the tool and invocation for the consecration of the tool and continue the Dark Moon Esbat with what follows next.

Dark Moon Esbat (Ending)

The ritual ends with Cakes and Wine. With arms upraised, say:

*I know of my needs and offer my appreciation to that
which sustains me. May I ever remember the blessings
of my Lady and my Lord.*

Lower arms and take up the goblet in the left hand and the knife in the right, slowly lower the point of the knife into the wine, and say:

*The Lord enters into the fruitful darkness of the Lady.
In Shadow is he and Shadow is she. The womb is the
tomb but the tomb is her womb, let me never forget that*

the light is reached through the dark, and she is the
passage I must follow as he follows for life's sake.

Remove the knife and set it on the altar. Take a drink from the cup and set it back on the altar. Touch the knife to the cake (or bread) and say:

The food of the dead and the Underworld is food of the
soul, let this cake be a symbol of the feeding of my spirit
as well as my body, that I may be whole in both.

Eat all but a little portion of the cake and drink all but a small amount of the wine for the final libation (gift to the deities to honor them), which, because it is Dark Moon, comes after the Practitioner's drink and symbolizes the final passage from life into death with the libation as Promise for new life from the Crone's cauldron.

When finished, hold the knife over the altar and say:

Lord and Lady, I am blessed by your sharing this time
with me; watching and guarding me, guiding me here
and in all things. I came in love and I depart in love.

Add the small portion of remaining cake and wine into the cauldron as the final libation, hold the cauldron aloft and say:

The remains of this life are passed into the cauldron for
this is the Promise: into death does all life pass to be
refreshed and move into life anew. The cauldron brings
life out of death. I honor the Lady and the Lord, who
bring light and life through darkness and death. The
dance is evermoving and neverending. So Mote It Be.

Set the cauldron down and raise the knife in a salute and say:

Love is the law and the bond. Merry did we meet,
merry do we part, and merry will we meet again.
Merry meet, merry part, and merry meet again!
The circle is now cleared. So Mote It Be!

Kiss the blade of the knife and set it on the altar. Take up the candle snuffer and go around the circle widdershins to snuff the candles at the Quarters, stopping at each point to address the Elemental by raising your arms and saying:

Depart in peace, Elemental Earth! We have met in kinship, thee and me. My blessings take with you!

Lower arms, envision the Elemental leaving, snuff the candle, and move to the next Quarter until all four Elementals are farewelled. Return to the altar and set down the snuffer. Raise your arms and say:

Beings and Powers of the visible and invisible, depart in peace! You aid in my work, whisper in my mind, bless me from realms of Shadow and Otherworld, and there is harmony between us. My blessings take with you. The circle is cleared.

Take the knife and go to the North Quarter, proceed deosil (N-E-S-W) around the circle envisioning the blue light being drawn back into the knife as you say:

The circle is open, yet the circle remains as its magical power is drawn back into me.

Upon reaching the North again, touch the flat of the knife blade against your forehead and envision the blue light swirling around and back into you. Return to the altar, raise up the knife and say:

The ritual is ended. Blessings have been given and blessings have been received. May the peace of the Goddess and the God remain in my heart. So Mote It Be!

Set the knife down and put away your tools.

The libation cauldron is poured into a depression in the ground and covered over (or a large flowerpot of soil can be used).

3

Who Are the Elementals?

The Elemental Presence

In working magics, conducting rituals, or engaging in ritual meditation, the Elementals are called on in setting up the circle and consecrating items. Afterwards they are farewelled with blessings given and received. But who are they? What are they? As I have formally practiced the Craft over the past thirty-five years, my understanding of the Elementals includes a feeling of *presence*. These are archetypes of the God and the Goddess expressed as individual entities and powers. As such, they are more than mere energies or servants that can be sent for and dismissed. They are not simply guardians who come and go, and they are not only the four elements of earth, air, fire, and water.

Green Witchcraft contains the ancient approach of *elementalism*, which is sometimes loosely defined as the worship of the elements as deities. This is not entirely accurate. Rather than being worshipped or seen as deities in their own right, up there with Zeus and the gang at Olympus, in the Green level of witchcraft, the Elementals are *emanations* of the Divine Power. Worship is not actually involved in the Craft so much as connection. It is a fine difference. Worship tends to require forms and dogmas, adherence to specific holy days, and rituals applied to these days of observance. This exists in the Green Craft as the Sabbats and Esbats, but the celebration is not mandatory nor is it required that the form remain consistent.

The Elementals themselves represent groups of fours. They are the earth, air, fire, and water, but also the cardinal directions of north, east, south, and west. They are colors as well—green, yellow, red, and blue—and they represent the seasons of winter, spring, summer, and fall. In like manner, they represent the ages of human development as child, youth, middle age, and old age. The Elementals are also the human aspects of strength, intellect, will, and emotions, and are found as integrated with the individual as body, mind, heart, and body fluids (blood and water).

These delineations and views of the Elementals help the witch to focus the power through the Elemental into a magical working. The Elementals relate to the Practitioner as the foundation of All. You add your own spirit to Elemental magics. They are seen and felt in the close-knit ties of family relations, hence they are referred to in the Green Witchcraft as kith and kin. Often the four are grouped as twos for balance. Numerology comes into play, particularly when working with the Elementals, because your perspective of the importance of numbers and their interrelationships are translated into the craft work you are doing.

As fours, a unity of the Elementals, there is foundation, firmness, strength, and solid growth. With twos, there is balance of pairs and/or opposites, dualities, and unions. Elementals Earth and Water may be considered as aligned with or as aspects of the Lady, while Elementals Air and Fire are aligned with or aspects of the Lord. Yet even this may change. The Elementals flow. They are not locked into one alignment or another, but may be emanations of goddess or god aspects. Thus the delineations of the Elemental forms become crossed, but in all cases, they have and are powers.

Earth may be the goddess as harvest and bounty; the goddess as barrenness; and the power of the earth in upheaval. Water may be the goddess as love and nurturing; the goddess of the life-giving waters and the sea; and the power of the tempest and the storm. These are goddess images of Maiden and Mother and Crone, translating their powers through the Elementals of Earth and Water, but the god may also be found in these two aspects. Earth may be the god as wilderness protector and lord of animals; the god as underworld ruler; and the power of death and destruction. Water may be the god as sea and nourisher; and the power of squall and hurricane.

With the other two Elementals, the same swapping may occur, although Air and Fire are normally identified as aspects of the god. Air may be the god as the breath of life; the god as intellect; and the power of the mind. Fire may be the god as life-giving sun and forger of metal; the god as passion and battle rage; and the power of energy. Yet these Elementals present the essence of the goddess as well. Air may be the goddess as muse or the power of tornados. Fire may be the goddess as impassioned ideals or the power of erupting volcanos.

By connecting with the Elementals in nature and in the Craft, you will find the oneness of all things. This is accomplished by extension of the Self into all things. The power of the natural objects used in Green magics comes from the Elementals and is funneled through the witch. The rule of exchange continues here, so that to receive a gift, you must give a gift. This exchange *binds* or *connects* the power and links the Elemental to the giver so that a gift may be released in turn. It is like an exchange of energy and a unifying of energy to accomplish a goal. The gift that is given may be an object, a symbol, or a blessing, but what matters is the sensation that accompanies the gift given and the knowing that this will prompt a return gift.

In primitive cultures, the exchange of gifts leads to further exchanges, and sometimes the gifting accelerates to such an extreme that there is danger of one tribal leader overpowering another through a display of economic power. If the other leader is embarrassed by this, a war between the tribes might occur over a point of honor. My mother was always careful not to overdo in gifts. She felt that people would not appreciate it if you gave them something that they themselves could not afford. It put them into an inferior or subservient position, and made any exchange of gifts awkward and unpleasant.

In the Craft, the same applies. When seeking the aid of the Elementals in a magical project, it is not necessary to overdo the gift giving. A big display of gifting is not any more productive. The people of Java and Tibet create huge colorful displays of food which they parade around, then offer to the Divine for a variety of reciprocations. This is a community affair and represents hundreds or thousands of people in a single main petition (often accompanied by a number of little, individual ones). In witchcraft, the individual is conducting the magic alone or in a small group, so a big display is not needed, nor will it bring about any greater a response. In gifting, keep it simple for the best results.

With each spell or ritual conducted in the Green Craft, the Elementals are contacted in some form. Whether the Craft work calls upon the energies of the light or the dark powers, the key to successful Elemental alignment of aid is in the envisioning. For Earth, there is earth, trees, rocks, fields, forests, mountains, and four-legged animals like the bull, horse, and stag. For Air, there is wind, clouds, birds, butterflies, moths, and flying insects. For Fire, there is flame, molten magma, phosphorescence, lightning, lava, and the salamander (traditionally believed to be able to live in fire). Water may be envisioned as ocean, river, rain, spring, water table, pond, brook, and fish.

Determine what image of the Elemental is appropriate for what you are doing, then envision the form of the Elemental to fit the type of Craft work. With circle Quarters, the basic forms of bull, eagle, salamander, and dolphin may be used. A Dark Moon celebration or spell might use the forms of troll, will-o'-the-wisp, St. Elmo's fire, and siren. A Sidhe Moon ritual could use the forms of gnome, sprite, dragon, and mermaid. A dark power ritual could utilize those forms of the Elementals that exhibit raw, untamed, highly energized power—earthquake, tornado, volcanic eruption, and hurricane. Whatever form is used depends upon your receptiveness to that image. If trolls have an ancient pull on you, harkening to a rough, dusky, earth-dwelling entity, that image will work, but if all you think of is a cute picture you saw in a children's book long ago, or a little troll doll with long pink hair, you might have a problem using that image for the Elemental Earth.

Plan your work ahead of time as much as possible, or let your feelings flow to find the imagery that will work for you in any given situation. Some people use dragons all around the Quarters, but see different varieties. One darkly beautiful tarot deck, designed by Peter Pracownik and Terry Donaldson, is based on Elemental dragons.

When you are accustomed to working with the Elementals, you become aware of their closeness to you. They are dependable powers that you can address without a ritual or ceremony. You can let them know your needs and wants without speaking, or in a low whisper, and they will respond.

I was once shopping for a scarf to cover my crystal ball, but I wanted a particular scarf. I envisioned what I wanted—something with blacks and deep dark greens, golds, and printed with leaves, not quite transparent, not totally opaque—and communicated this to the Elementals. Then I went to a shop and began browsing their scarf rack. I pulled out the scarf I had envisioned—then in a playful mood, I addressed the Elementals and suggested a different image as I flicked my hand through the rack. That scarf appeared, and I took that one as well. Then, simply to be sure about what I was doing, I envisioned yet one more that I wanted, and there it appeared in my hand. By now I was laughing (as were they), and I told the Elementals that was quite enough as I was running up a bill. I had to force myself to not envision anything else.

The other point to consider, too, is that when you ask for something and get it, do not turn it down. In other words, the Elementals are happy to work for you, and will play with you, but they do not expect you to abuse the relationship. Incidentally, the same applies to Fairy gifts. When you receive an unexpected gift of nature, you can pretty much know the Other People are renewing their ties with you. Accept the gift. I have a wood box from Brazil with irridescent blue butterflies in a design under glass on the lid. I keep many of my Fairy gifts in there until such a time when I may need one.

In the next section, I describe an Elemental bottle and how to create one. This bottle becomes a tool of the Craft by relating the practitioner to the Elementals on a personal level. A close approach enhances your ability to work with the Elementals and through them, but the bottle is certainly not required to make this contact.

The Elementals are not always *invisible*. I awoke one night to see four shrouded forms in my room, their hands at their sides as they stood in a square around me. My first thought went to a Craft book I had recently read and the words on banishing unexpected spirit entities, but I decided as I observed them that such an action would be rude. That made me think about how I needed to explain to people that when you do magics, you don't have to be afraid of your helpers.

Then the squareness of their presence struck me as very meaningful, and I said, "Oh! You are the Four Elementals!" I was very tired, so I simply blessed them and told them I was going back to sleep. They raised their arms so that their hands touched in the center of their square over me, with their long, shadowy fingers opened, and I felt they returned the blessing. Then I went back to sleep. I know this happened because I had initially looked over at my husband and saw that he was sound asleep. Many years later, a very talented seeker told me about her strange experience after she had taken some classes from me. She awoke one night to see four shrouded figures. You know the rest! I had not told anyone about my incident, so I can certainly accept her own experience as genuine, and I am pleased that she calmly recognized who they were.

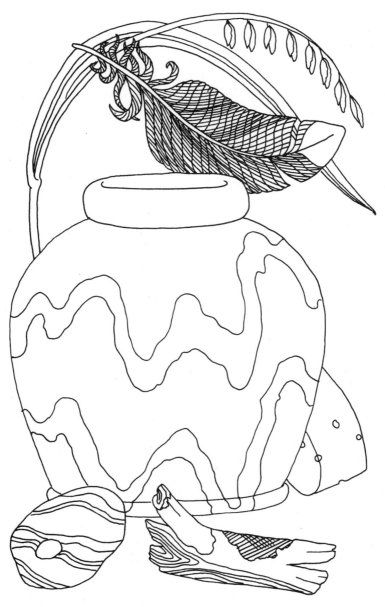

By connecting with the Elementals in nature and in the Craft, you will find the oneness of all things. This is accomplished by extension of the Self into all things. The power of the natural objects used in Green magics comes from the Elementals and is funneled through the witch.

— Ritual —
Creating an Elemental Bottle

An Elemental bottle is used to help you focus on the Elemental Powers of Earth, Air, Fire, and Water, and to alert them to your desire to work with them. They are in you and outside of you in various forms, so when you create the bottle using objects that relate to the Elementals, they also relate to you.

As you think about what you want to represent the Elementals, and if you have sought connection with the Other People, look for gifts from the Fair Folk for the bottle. These might include such things as feathers, shells, holey stones (stones with a naturally created hole in them), specially marked stones (white circles), Fairy money (flat stone disks with little markings), lava, pumice, and natural charred wood (lightning strike).

To make your own Elemental bottle, you could either make or purchase a suitable pottery bottle. Put the items you have selected as representative of the four Elementals on a table with the bottle. Now you are ready to dedicate the bottle to connection between yourself and the Elementals. Create your circle and call upon the Elementals. Raise up the bottle and show it to each of the Elementals at the Quarters and say as you turn:

> *Elementals form the jar as Earth and Air mixed with*
> *Water and Fire—so is the container of my spirit formed*
> *as this jar.*

Bless the Earth object with salt (or burdock root dust) and call upon that Elemental to bless the object "in remembrance of the union between thee and me"; then put it into the bottle. Bless the Air object with incense smoke and repeat the process. Bless the Fire object with (purple) candle flame repeating the procedure, then bless the Water object with spring water and repeat the process.

Now, cork the bottle. Use three 3-foot long strands of yarn—white, red, and black—to represent the Triple Goddess. Knot them together at one end and braid the strands. Wrap the completed braid around the cork in the bottle and secure (a slip knot works fine).

You can decorate the outside of the bottle with objects representing the Elementals, using the same method and words as before.

Bless the completed bottle and say:

> *Elementals within and Elementals without; as this*
> *container is my body, we are united as Kith and Kin in*
> *love and respect, one to the other, Thy power within me,*
> *around me, and at one with me, with blessings given*
> *and blessings received. So Mote It Be.*

Store the bottle on your personal altar, shrine, or other place where you do your magical workings, or simply where it can be seen and will act as a reminder of the union between you as a practitioner and the Elementals in kinship.

4

What Are the Dark Powers?

Archetypes

The dark powers emanate from the dark aspects of the Goddess and the God. This is the power of the Crone and the Lord of Shadows; the Hag and the Hunter. The dark powers are more than just a personification of the negative influences in life, however, and the energy raised through the dark imagery of the Divine is very potent. As such, you must use care in what you do. *Be careful what you do.*

The Dark Goddess is manifested in mythology as various kinds of death crones, wise hags, devastation, war, disease, and barrenness of the land. The Dark God is seen in mythologies as the silent host to the dead in his underground realm of gray shadows and deep sleep, knowing of secrets and wise of the universe, death, war, destruction, gatherer of souls, and harbinger of chaos.

She is the Bone Mother who collects the skulls of the dead for the ossuary. This is the ingathering of the material remains of the life that was. He is the Hunter, whose rade (Wild Hunt) ingathers the energies of the soul. There is sense to this ancient cosmology that does not touch on fear. Indeed, the mystery cults of ancient times focused on the dark aspects of the Divine so that their followers would move past their fear of mortality to seize upon the recognition of their eternal immortality.

As a power, the Dark Lord is the Chaos from which Order must evolve. Yet since there is no ending to this cycle, Order resolves again into Chaos, to be reborn as a New Order. The Lord of Shadows as Death becomes the process of new life by gathering the energy of dying life, and the Passage into a new material form is through the Crone.

In the aspect of light, the god dies willingly by entering the ground to bring his vitality to the crops that will be harvested later to feed humanity. Through his selfless act, he revitalizes the earth. He does this through the Crone. The marriage of Lugh in August, celebrated as the Sabbat, Lughnassadh, is the start of the god's descent into Mother Earth. Once there, he is transformed into the son within the goddess. Hence, the pagan god is both Father and Son, which is why Christianity could readily blend with local paganism and absorb the pagan holidays. The harvest comes, the seasons change, and the Mother becomes the Crone of fall and winter, only to be transformed into Mother again at Winter Solstice with the rebirth of the Sun (her son, the god).

The womb-tomb is the domain of the Crone and is a place of great power. This is where transformation takes place, with the energies of death given repose and returned to form as the energies of life. When this power is confronted and recognized, there comes a freedom from fear, a new sense of independence, and a recognition of personal responsibility. We are not judged in death by the Lady and the Lord, but we are Self-judged. From the quietude of his realm we move through her into new life. That is the balanced, pagan theme of the cauldron, the god of self-sacrifice, and the resurrecting goddess. It is this power of the goddess that significantly differentiates the old and new religions.

Thus, in the historical sense, while the Dark Lord guides the chaos of social and cultural changes through the Crone into a new life, the Crone becomes not the terror of death, but the joyful passage to new vibrant societies through the death of the outmoded and stagnant ones. She is Fata Morgana (Morgan the Fate), the Huntress Diana, Minerva, Cerridwen, Sati, and Kali. He is Pluto, Hades, Cernunnos, Herne the Hunter, Set, and Shiva, but the names may not convey the image needed by the practitioner unless you are able to move beyond the modern association of darkness as evil.

In the Green Craft, the numbers two and four seem to have special significance time and again. I can only speculate as to the cause, but I suspect this relates to the sense of balance and grounding offered through witchcraft. There are two deities of light—a goddess and a god—and two deities of darkness—a goddess and a god. But these deities are the same, so a square of four is created by the two sets of twos, because the god and the goddess are united in the form of androgyne, the four equal one. These are significant numbers in the Green Craft and represent balance, strength, and unity. There is one other number to come.

By accepting that the dark powers are in balance with the light powers, you are able to utilize the wholeness of the Power. The dichotomy of good and evil do not apply to what simply is. Energy can be drawn to the light or to the dark; thus death provides the soul's passage to whichever realm the soul-energy has been drawn. Energy is always in motion, and flows back and forth between light and dark. What at one time is light energy turns and becomes dark energy. Through the practice of the Craft, the witch directs this energy for a beneficial purpose. To do otherwise is to inflict Self-harm. *What you send comes back.*

To face the Underworld and the power of the dark aspect of the Divine is to understand that dark is part of the necessary balance of life and not something to fear. The unifying of the dark and the light within the individual offers wholeness and peace, which may then be transferred to external contacts.

Dark Powers in Witchcraft

The Sabbats of witchcraft relate to the solar seasons as Quarters, and to agricultural cycles as Cross-Quarters. The Esbats celebrate the phases of the Moon, normally Full and New. These days of observance emphasize the unity of Sun-Earth-Moon-Witch found in the rituals and workings of the Craft. Some of these holy days are light-sided, others are dark-sided. In the Sabbats, Lughnassadh is the cross-over point into darkness for the god when he begins the journey to new light at Yule.

From Yule to Lughnassadh, the energies of the Earth are reviving as the growing relationship between the Lady and the Lord, culminating in mating in Beltane, and moving to the willing sacrifice of the Lord in August. The first harvest is the Bread Harvest of August, when the Lord descends into the Lady—Mother Earth—to give his life-essence, the Solar energy, into the grain to feed the children of the Earth. The second harvest is in September—once called Harvest Home, it is now the Sabbat of Mabon. This was the Vine Harvest and was celebrated with much festivity and wine. These two festivals annually celebrate the offered body and blood of the god, a theme found throughout the pagan world of ancient times.

Dedicated to the Dark Lord are the Sabbats of Lughnassadh, Mabon, and Samhain; he then changes overnight from Holly King to Oak King at Yule. Yule is the second crossover that the Lord makes, moving from Underworld back to the Earth. He descends into the Earth at Lughnassadh and spreads his body into the crops, then at Mabon he pours out his blood into the vines. At Samhain, he is in his realm of Underworld, awaiting the Crone, who comes to him and receives him back into herself to be born again at Yule when she transforms into the Holy Mother, and he into her newborn son.

The Dark Lord and the Crone meet as equals in darkness at Samhain—when all is Hallows in this world, Underworld, and Otherworld—when their transformation forms a moment in time that allows the inhabitants of the worlds to come into close contact. The veil between the worlds is thinnest at Samhain; this is the time to honor your ancestors, greet passing spirits, and seek answers to your questions from beyond the physical plane.

On All Hallows Eve (Halloween) lighted gourds or turnips serve as guides for the spirits in the night. Salt, bread, and beer (mead), wine, or water are set at an empty place at the table for the departed loved ones to return for a visit. Apples or pomegranates are buried in the yard to give sustenance to passing spirits. This is a time for divinations, future scrying, and conversing with the Shadowland. It is also the moment when the God passes from the Tomb into the Womb.

Dark Moons

With Moon phases, the Goddess as Maiden is celebrated at the waxing crescent, as Mother at full, and as Crone at the waning crescent. These phases make up the typical symbol of the Triple Goddess in witchcraft. However, even in this emblem, the reverse side of the Full Moon portion is the Hidden Face, or Fourth Aspect of the Goddess—the Dark Moon. The waning crescent honors the Crone of wisdom and age, but the Dark Moon is the Goddess as Tomb and Womb. It is the place where the God enters at Lughnassadh to rule as Lord of Shadows. Meditations rather than magics are normally practiced on the night of the Dark Moon. It is a time for contemplating and uniting with the mysteries of the Dark Aspect of the Divine.

Ordinarily, magic work during the Dark Moon is not likely to be very successful simply because this phase signifies the quiet time, the sleep or dreamtime, of post- or pre-embodiment. The rest of Death is celebrated now—the comfort of being embraced by the Lady and the Lord of Shadows for a quiet moment—no magic spellwork calling on them for power, no Calling Down of the Goddess, but reverie and comprehension of the Passage through Death. This is the silent power that exists after death and prior to rebirth. It is the moment of being received into the Underworld and the moment of departure from the Shadowland to be reborn into the world. It is a time of change and transition that is suited best for dark power magics.

By visualizing that there are two sets of Quarters for the Divine—the Quarters in Light and the Quarters in Dark—the number eight becomes significant. Until you reach the point of acceptance of the dark as in balance with the light, your work remains in twos, fours, and one, but the completion in Green Witchcraft is naturally enough a duality of fours. The number eight is interpreted as dual foundations, the new built upon the old— hence, order and law. That is why there are Rules of Conduct rather than a rede or charge. The Rules address working with both the light and the dark powers.

Fairy Moon

There is also the Other Moon phase, which is the phenomenon of two Dark Moons in one solar month. Such an occurrence is not common, yet happened in February and again in March of 1995. When there are two Full Moons in the same solar month, the second one is referred to as a Blue Moon. These generally occur in August. This is the best time to give extra power to magics and spells involving creativity, expression, and productivity. Like the Blue Moon, the Other Moon enhances a particular variety of magical practice.

The Other Moon is the reflection in this world of the Full Moon in the Otherworld. It is a glimpse into that realm from behind the Moon of the Other People, and so it is also called the Sidhe or Fairy Moon. When the Sidhe Moon shines, the witch has the opportunity to conduct the dark magics that call on the Fairy powers, and seek the aid of the Sidhe. These are Fairy magics, familiar magics, and companion magics. The companion may be honored at this time, or one may be sought now if the witch does not yet have such a friend. This Moon may be a like a holiday time for the companion—a time to visit home, and perhaps bring the witch along.

Journeys

The Sidhe Moon ritual that follows (beginning on page 61) should only be used if you feel comfortable in heart, mind, body, and spirit about intermingling with the Other People. A certain strength is required, lest the practitioner fall into the yearning that often accompanies Otherworldly contact. A common Fairy motif is the pining away of one who has been to Otherworld.

This ritual is more suited for solitary rather than group activity as the magics are externalized only minimally. This is when the witch, rather than standing between the worlds, enters Otherworld. The modern incorporation of shamanism into Wicca comes from relating this witchcraft element of transition into Otherworld to the later development of the shamanic journey. The difference between these forms of practice lies in the purpose. For the shaman, the spirit of someone who is dying is being fought for, but for the witch, the journey is one of communion and interaction.

Often a Companion from Otherworld comes into a person's life through dreams. The Companion may be encountered during astral travel, or may be discovered within a Fairy Crystal—look into the crystal to see who is there.

— Ritual —
Sidhe Moon Ritual and Companion Quest

While the New Moon honors the Dark Aspect of the Goddess as Crone, and the Dark Moon is held in hallowed reverence of the Goddess as the Tomb of Rebirth, the Sidhe Moon enhances magical practice with Otherworld.

The black mirror is an excellent tool in the seeking of a Companion from Otherworld (see "Consecrating a Dark Aspect Tool" in the "Dark Moon Ritual," in Chapter 2). Often such a Companion comes into a person's life through dreams—and is constantly there, sometimes helping in a situation, sometimes observing, sometimes stepping in at a crucial point. The Companion may be encountered during astral travel, or may be discovered within a Fairy Crystal (fluorite crystal with a combination of purple, green, and gray tones). If buying such a crystal in order to find a Companion, look into the crystal first to see who is there—the crystal is like a doorway into Otherworld—and if the person (or people) seen within appear(s) interested in being with you, then get the crystal. If there is no one to be seen, or the person seems disinterested, leave it for someone else.

Some people consider Companions to be spirit guides, but there are different sensations involved between guides and Companions. While the spirit guides are normally other people from the present or past life who have passed on but have returned to watch over someone they love, the Companions are from Otherworld and have a very different feel about them. The Companion Quest can be conducted at any time during the Waning Moon, for this is the Waxing Moon of Otherworld, but the Sidhe Moon is the best time for optimum results on this quest.

To prepare for a Companion Quest, set up a table, and place two chairs on opposite sides of the table (East and West), in the area where the ritual will be conducted. Lay a clean cloth (lace or cotton) of white, purple, or gray on the table. Place a gray pillar candle at the center of the table and set the black mirror behind it so that when you sit at the table, you will be in the East chair, the candle will be visible to you, the mirror will be behind the candle, and the

Guest's chair will be the West chair. Have the ritual knife on the table and a wand of elderwood (although hazel or hawthorn will also do well), along with a small bowl of spring water, diced burdock root, and an incense that is earthy, green, or misty in scent. Set out two small bowls (natural hollow stones or seed pods are excellent), one for flowers (without the stems) or flower petals and one for milk, on the table at the East side where you will stand, and set out a dish containing a tablespoon to a quarter cup of dried mugwort. A candle snuffer will also be needed.

The meals taken during the day of the ritual may consist of fruits, berries, grains, dairy products, roots, tubers, leaves, and fresh-water fish, or game—no "domesticated" meat, poultry, or seafood. This diet will aid in attuning to Otherworld as these are foods commonly attributed in mythology and tradition as favored by the Other People.

Take a nocturnal bath in a room (bathroom) scented with patchouli incense and lighted with one to three gray candles. The bath water should be infused with an herb bag of heather, lavender, linden (tila), marigold (calendula), and rosemary. After the bath, dress lightly and comfortably, then brew a pot of Fairy Tea. The tea is used to set the mood and to draw upon the powers of the herbs to attract the attention of the Other People.

Fairy Tea

Combine in a teapot:

3	teaspoons black tea	1½	teaspoon hops
½	teaspoon chamomile	½	teaspoon mugwort
1	teaspoon dandelion root	½	teaspoon raspberry leaf
½	teaspoon elder flower	1½	teaspoon rose hips

Then say as you drop the herbs into the pot:

> *Black for power, apple of night, root of the sun, Lady's blessing, Lord's leap for joy, then between the worlds, to Fairy bramble, with token of love, brewed to bring Fair Ones close to me.*

Boil water in a kettle and add to the teapot. Let steep for five minutes. Warm a second teapot by swirling inside it the remaining hot water. Pour out the water and strain the brewed tea into this warmed pot. Take the tea things (pot, sweetener, and milk) and two cups to the ritual table and set them out for yourself and your Guest. Add a plate with cookies or tea biscuits (the Scottish shortbread is very good and can be found in most supermarkets). Set out a bowl of flowers and a bowl of milk on the table at the East side where you will stand.

Draw the circle and call upon the Elementals using the imagery of the Sidhe Moon Ritual. Stand at the East side of the table so you are facing West (do not sit down yet). You will probably want to have some pleasant music that you enjoy playing softly in the background. This will help the people of Otherworld to focus on you and gain an insight to what you are like. Light patchouli incense for an earthy scent or use an incense evocative of green earth or rain. The names used here for the Lady and Lord of Fairy are only suggestions; you may use whatever comes to you or has resonance to you.

Sidhe Moon Ritual

Sweep the circle deosil (N-E-S-W) with the besom (but *not* one made of broom or Scotch Broom since the Fair Ones find the odor of broom offensive: straw, grasses, pine needles or boughs, leaves, etc. is fine), and say:

> *As I sweep this circle, may it be cleansed and made ready for my work.*

Candles are set at the Quarters (North, East, South, and West): pale green candles should be used at the North and South; and gray candles at the East and West. Alternatively, four crystals or stones may be placed at the Quarters. Light the incense and the pillar candle, then clap your hands three times, and say:

> *The circle is about to be cast and I freely stand within to greet the Other People with the blessing of my Lady and my Lord of Greenwood.*

If using candles at the Quarters, light them by taking the pillar candle around to each Quarter candle, moving widdershins, beginning at the West (W-S-E-N), and saying:

> *I call upon the Light between the Waters to illuminate and protect the circle* (envision the glowing mists that rise from rivers at night).

South:

> *I call upon the Light between the Fires to illuminate and protect the circle* (envision the blue glow of the will-o'-the-wisp dancing through a dense marsh).

East:

> *I call upon the Light between the Airs to illuminate and protect the circle* (envision the sparkling blue flames of ball lightning—dancing between sky and ground).

North:

> *I call upon the Light between the Earths to illuminate and protect the circle* (envision the glow of river hyacinth at night or the pale green of phosphorescent light in caverns).

If using crystals or stones at the Quarters, move around the circle in the same manner, except raise up the candle before each stone or crystal and use the same invocation. Return to the table and set the candle back in its place, then take up the knife and say:

> *I draw this circle in the presence of the Lady and the Lord of Otherword to be a place where the Other People may manifest and bless me who am their Sister/Brother in this world and known as* _____ (Craft Name).

Move around the circle widdershins (W-S-E-N) with the knife lowered, envision a blue light shooting from the knife's tip to form the circle boundary and say:

> *This is the boundary of the circle in which only love*
> *shall enter and leave.*

Return to the table and put the tip of the knife into the dish of diced burdock root and say:

> *Spring water is the purity of the Lady and the Fount of*
> *Life Eternal; burdock is the Lord's root of purification,*
> *protection, and warding of the negative. I bless this*
> *water and root to be used in the circle in the names of*
> *the Lady and the Lord, the Queen and the King of*
> *Otherworld* (can use Mab and Fearn or Titania and
> Oberon, etc.).

Touch the water with the tip of the knife and say:

> *In the names of the Lady and the Lord of Otherworld, I*
> *consecrate and cleanse this water to be used in this circle.*

Take the consecrated water bowl and, moving W-S-E-N, sprinkle water from it around the circle, and say:

> *I consecrate this circle in the names of* (the Queen and
> King of Fairy). *This circle is conjured a Circle of Power*
> *that is purified and sealed.*

Return the bowl to the table, take up the incense, and move around the circle (W-S-E-N) to cense it, then return it to the table. Put a drop of the water on your fingertip, make a Solar Cross on your forehead, then a Lunar Spiral over this, and say:

> *I, _____* (Craft Name), *am consecrated before the Lady*
> *and Lord of Otherworld, in this their circle.*

Take the wand and address the Elementals at their Quarters of the circle where the candles are, holding the wand aloft with arms open at each site, and say at the appropriate Quarter (W-S-E-N):
West:

> *I call upon you, Elemental Water, to attend this rite and*
> *guard this circle, for as I have blood and feelings, we*
> *are kith and kin!*

65

South:

I call upon you, Elemental Fire, to attend this rite and guard this circle, for as I have the spark of life and strength of will, we are kith and kin!

East:

I call upon you, Elemental Air, to attend this rite and guard this circle, for as I have breath and thought, we are kith and kin!

North:

I call upon you, Elemental Earth, to attend this rite and guard this circle, for as I have body and fortitude, we are kith and kin!

For Elemental envisionings, you might see a mermaid for Water, a will-o'-the-wisp for Fire, Fairies or sylphs for Air, and gnomes or cobalts for Earth, but these are only suggestions and you should use what comes to you.

Return to the table and use the wand to draw the symbol of Infinity (an 8 laying on its side) in the air above the altar—this is the symbol of working between the worlds. With the wand in both hands, raise it over your head and say:

Hail to the Elementals at the Four Quarters! Welcome Lady and Lord to this rite! I stand between the worlds with love and power all around! I call upon my Lady and my Lord as Queen and King of the Sidhe to bless my communion with the Other People. I affirm my joy of union with the Divine in all realms and worlds, and I acknowledge your blessings upon me. What I send returns to me, and I conduct my Craft accordingly.

Set down the wand and pick up the knife. Hold it over the teapot and say:

Great Lady, bless this creature of Water and of Earth to your service. May I always remember the cauldron

66

waters of rebirth and the many forms of being.
Of Water and Earth am I.

Set the knife on the table, hold up the teapot, and say:

I honor you, Great Lady!

Replace the teapot on the table and pick up the wand, then hold it over the incense and say:

Great Lord, bless this creature of Fire and Air to your
service. May I always remember the sacred fire that
dances within all life and hear the voices of the Divine.
Of Fire and Air am I.

Set the wand on the table, hold up the censer, and say:

I honor you, Great Lord!

Return the censer to the table. Pour a small amount of tea into your cup (do not add anything to it) and say:

Power and Grace, Beauty and Strength are in the
Lady and the Lord. Patience and Love, Wisdom and
Knowledge, you are Endings, Passages, and Begin-
nings, in all worlds are you. I honor you both!

Pour a bit of tea from the cup into the bowl of flowers and take a sip from the cup. Stand facing West, raise arms in an open gesture, and say:

Hail to the People of the Land of Mist. Greetings I send
to the People of the Undying Lands of Otherworld.
Hear my call and let the Gateway be opened between
This World and Otherworld. In the names of the Lady
and the Lord, (Mab and Fearn, or Titania and Oberon, etc.), *do I call upon the Fair Ones in peace and love.*

Lower arms, carefully lift the gray pillar candle, and say:

As this light shines before me, let the light of
Otherworld reach into this place.

Here you may insert the Companion Call or continue the ritual by modifying the section as a time of meditation and a ritual meal.

Companion Quest

Set the candle on the table and move to the West side of the table, pull the chair aside a bit so one who wishes to come may be seated, then move back to the East side of the table. Add a bit of the mugwort to the gray candle—enough to smolder, but not to put out the candle (if it does go out, simply relight it, no harm done). Be seated, look into the black mirror beyond the candle flame, and say:

> *Here lies the doorway into Otherworld; I welcome my*
> *guest through this portal.*

Gaze into the mirror for a time and envision a misty, fog-shrouded forest; feel the cool, refreshing air; smell the damp leaves on the forest floor, the moss on the ancient large trees; hear the sound of water gurgling along a narrow brook; hear the soft, delicate, hesitant footfalls of a browsing deer; and listen for the quiet steps of Another approaching through the dark forest, coming toward you; and when you see Another gazing back, lift up (one in each hand) the bowls of flowers and milk, and greet your Guest:

> *Hail to thee and blessed be thy feet that brought you*
> *on this path; blessed be thy heart that beats steadfast;*
> *blessed be thy eyes that see between the worlds; blessed*
> *be thy hands offered in friendship and clasped in mine.*

Set the bowls in front of either side of the tea setting for the Guest, then offer your hands together, palms up, and bend your fingers toward your palm as you greet your Visitor; release the handclasp, and prepare to serve tea. The forest will remain in view behind your Visitor so that the table will appear to be partly in woodland; the sounds of forest animals and the brook will continue in the background. Introduce yourself and say,

> *I am honored by your presence, and you are welcome at*
> *this table set between the worlds.*

Now serve tea for both places, adding sugar and milk, and a biscuit on the edge of each saucer (the food and drink of the Other is not consumed in the material manner, but the flavor essence will be removed). Then with arms opened, palms up, bless the meal by saying this or something similar:

> *I know of my needs and offer my appreciation to that*
> *which sustains me. May I ever remember the blessings of*
> *my Lady and my Lord. The Lord brings spiritual life*
> *through the bounty of the Lady of Otherworld, that all is*
> *created in undying beauty. I honor the inner beauty of*
> *the spirit.*

You may drink tea and eat with your Guest, and simply visit with your Guest silently and talk about your desire for a Companion from the Otherworld to aid, guide, work and walk with you. Add more mugwort to the candle from time to time to keep the aroma in the air. When finished, and if you are so inclined, ask your Guest to be your Companion and to find a crystal to use as passage to you that you may carry with you (if there is not one in your possession already, you will encounter it soon; look inside it and see your friend—it does not contain or imprison the Other, but is a window into Otherworld and a gateway to you). When finished, stand and say:

> *I am blessed by your having shared this tea with me.*
> *My blessings I give to thee. We came in friendship and*
> *depart in friendship. Merry we meet, merry we part,*
> *and merry we will meet again. Merry meet, merry*
> *part, merry meet again.*

Envision your Guest standing when you stand; extend your hand again, palm up, and feel the cool touch of the Other's hand in farewell. Sit before the candle and mirror and envision the misty forest becoming darker; the quiet footfalls of the departing Guest disappear into the wildwood; the splashing water of the brook becomes fainter; the deer bounds off into the depths of the wood; the forest disappears, and the door closes; you are looking into the black mirror and see yourself looking back.

Sidhe Moon Ritual Conclusion

Pick up the knife, hold it over the table, and say:

*Lady and Lord of the Sidhe, I am blessed by your
sharing this time with me. Watch over and guard me,
guide me here and on all my paths. I came in love and
I depart in love. I honor the Lady and the Lord of
Otherworld, where the spirit is nourished in song and
joy. The dance is evermoving and neverending.
So Mote It Be.*

Raise the knife in a salute and say:

*Love is the Law and the Bond. Merry did we meet,
merry do we part, and merry will we meet again.
Merry meet, merry part, and merry meet again!
The circle is now cleared. So Mote It Be!*

Kiss the blade of the knife and set it on the table. Take up the candle snuffer and go around the circle to snuff the candles at the Quarters, stopping at each point to address the Elemental by raising your arms and saying:

Depart in peace, Elemental Water (Earth, Fire, Air),
and my blessings take with you!

Lower your arms, envision the Elemental leaving, snuff the candle and move to the next Quarter until all four have been bidden farewell. Return to the table and set down the snuffer. Raise your arms and say:

*Beings and Powers of the visible and invisible, depart in
peace! You aid in my work, whisper in my mind, bless
me from all realms and worlds you inhabit, and there is
harmony between us. My blessings take with you.
The circle is cleared.*

Take the knife and go to the North Quarter, proceed deosil (N-E-S-W) around the circle, envisioning the blue light being drawn back into the knife as you say:

The circle is open, yet the circle remains as its magical power is drawn back into me.

When reaching the North again, touch the flat of the knife blade against your forehead and envision the blue light swirling around and back into you. Return to the altar, raise up the knife and say:

The ritual is ended. Blessings have been given and blessings have been received. May the peace of the Goddess and the God remain in my heart. So Mote It Be!

When you have found the Companion crystal, it can be placed on your altar when not being carried by you. By placing a dish of flowers and a dish of milk on the altar with the crystal, you are honoring and refreshing your Friend in Otherworld. Up until recent times, stone depressions in Sweden were used as receptacles for milk and flowers to honor the Elves, and this tradition is echoed in Celtic lands by the leaving of a bowl of milk and crust of bread outside the door for the Fairy Folk.

Black Mirror Passage

Using a similar ritual format, one can pass through the mirror's doorway into Otherworld with the Companion. In this case, it is not that the person feels the movement into the mirror so much as it is that the forest comes to the person and moves behind. Do not look back (a traditional injunction in mythology) or you will propel yourself back through the gateway, which the Other People may find annoying.

Perfect love and perfect trust are required in order for the passage and visit to be a smooth one. Enjoy the sights, sounds, sensations, and atmosphere of Otherworld, and your Guide will bring you back to the portal, which will appear as a dark spot surrounded by forest. As you approach the spot, it gets larger, until you are near enough for it to be a doorway, then you turn to say farewell to your Companion, and with your back to the doorway, the forest will recede around you until it is in front of you and behind the mirror, and then fades away completely. Then you may close the door and open the circle.

— Meditation —
Past Lives Meditation*

The powers of the Dark Lady and Dark Lord can be used to reveal the secrets of the past through a black mirror meditation. This type of meditation may be used on its own or in conjunction with a dark aspect ritual such as a Dark Moon Esbat or a Sidhe Moon Esbat.

Feel free to incorporate your own ideas for a more rewarding experience. After all, one person's visualization is not the same as your own, so while another's meditation may be enjoyable, perceptions are individualized. It is fine to alter and personalize a published meditation to make it more meaningful. If music is used during the meditation, it should be chosen to supplement and not overpower the mood being set. I recommend keeping the music very low to avoid interfering with your mental focus.

A Dark Moon Esbat ritual may be used in conjunction with a black mirror meditation, although the meditation may be done without the Esbat ritual. It is a matter of preference. The meditation may be used alone by creating a circle and calling upon the Elementals to guard the sacred space, using Dark Moon Esbat imagery.

A black mirror may be purchased at most Craft stores, mail ordered, or made by the individual. Prior to use, wash it in water infused with mugwort, dry it, and consecrate it at both the Full Moon and the Dark Moon so the mirror can be used for a variety of meditations and spellwork. Smoothed and polished obsidian also makes an excellent meditation tool, especially if you can find one that fits comfortably in the palm of your hand. If a tool will be used for Otherworld meditations, it should be not be consecrated with salt but with burdock root.

Be seated either before the altar where this is done as part of a ritual or at a table that can be used for this meditation.

Light a black candle (votive, pillar, or stick) in its holder, using the center altar candle, and say:

This candle glows to light the path into Darkness.

---

* Previously published in *Llewellyn's 1998 Magical Almanac*. Reprinted with permission.

Place the candle in front of the propped-up black mirror (you may want to drum or shake a gourd rattle against the palm of your hand as you chant).

> *I call upon the Dark and the Past; the Ancient of*
> *Days in the Realm of Repast. Unleash to my sight the*
> *paths I have roamed; and show me the forms of lives I*
> *have known.*

Look past the candle and into the mirror to gaze into your own eyes.

Continue to shake the gourd and chant the rhyme, without really listening to it or paying attention to the motion; focus on the mirror and watch as the face changes into those of past lives.

Do not be surprised to see faces of the opposite sex or even of beings not guessed at or known. The soul's journey encompasses the Universe, and where one has resided may be other than Earth. In some cases you may even see a progression of lives into other life forms of Earth. Not all lives need be considered from the past, as some may be yet to come, or are on other planes; the location of the past depends upon one's location on the spiral at any given moment.

When done, if still shaking the gourd, stop and say:

> *The memories of past and future are shown; the faces*
> *of me in Time are now known. Blessings I give to the*
> *Veiled One of Night; for through this mask am I given*
> *the Sight.*

Cover the mirror with a black cloth and snuff the candle.

Proceed with the Esbat ritual or take some refreshment and move back into a normal routine.

5

How Are the Dark Powers Used?

Meditation

I n order to use the dark powers in witchcraft, a certain amount of creativity is needed. Meditations help develop that ability, and so does that bugaboo of teachers—daydreaming. Practical daydreaming allows you to put yourself into situations and apply a variety of responses until you find one that works when the situation is played out. Even children's programming on television uses this approach in teaching children how to imagine what will happen as a result of their actions. As we grow older, this notion of helpful daydreaming is discouraged in society as a thing meant for children. Often, meditation stimulates a dormant creative process.

The Rules of Conduct, outlined earlier, act as a guide to help a person practice the ancient arts without harm to self or others. In calling upon the dark powers, the goal must not be an increase of anger or rage, nor an intent to do harm. When you are connected to the Divine and ask for harm to another, you are really saying that you feel a need for self-punishment. Some people seek this as a means of compensating for prior actions—a way of mitigating accumulated karma from past lives or this life so that it is not a burden in the next incarnation.

Columnist Ann Landers talks about turning life's lemons into lemonade, and my mother used to tell me when I was angry or upset, to "turn it around." Her instruction to me was to take a different perspective on any given situation. Our culture attempts to lump things into dichotomies of good and bad, light and dark, but reality is grays and shadows. There is a universe of options available, it is simply a matter of discovering what you really want.

Instead of saying, for example, "I want to make so and so suffer for hurting my feelings," you need to examine why your feelings were hurt and determine how to deal with that cause.

Through meditation, you can connect with all aspects of the earth as part of a cohesive entity—animal, mineral, plant, water, clouds, sky, and so forth. It becomes, then, a primary step to your union with the cosmos—space, the stars, comets, planets, asteroids, black holes, pulsars, and so forth. You can use meditation to journey to other worlds, other dimensions, and other planes of existence in spectrums ordinarily overlooked or out of reach.

Meditation helps you open your awareness to achieve alternative states of being and enhance learning. You can promote good health by calming your mind and soothing your nervous system. A lot of stomach, intestinal, and cardiac problems can be traced to mental and emotional states. When you are overwrought, meditating helps your physical body by relieving those tensions that are being physically manifested.

Some of the ways that your body expresses distress due to mental or emotional stress are through a nervous stomach, intestinal discomfort, colitis, ulcers, hives, and rashes. With extreme anger, vision can become impaired, heart palpitations can occur, and breathing difficulties may be experienced. The nausea of the anxious person or the flushed face of the angry person has no detrimental or negating effect on the cause—it only adds to personal discomfort and perhaps to serious, life-threatening physical reactions.

How Meditation Works

Meditation gives you a chance to switch off the routine consciousness that chatters in your head in endless circles of fear, guilt, recrimination, or anger—rehashing events that have a negative effect on your mental and emotional health. This switching off allows your subconscious mind, your intuitive Self, to take over and address a problem from a new, more cosmic perspective. By moving into an alternative state of awareness, other worlds or realms may be visited, knowledge or information gathered and brought back with you to enhance your conscious life.

When you meditate regularly, you will learn to move with ease between the worlds whenever you wish. With practice, you may find that you are able to reside in multiple worlds at the same time. This latter phenomenon can lead to some very interesting experiences. You are literally able to manifest your subconscious.

The steps for meditation have already been discussed in the exercise in Chapter 1. Find a quiet place to sit where you will not be interrupted for twenty to thirty minutes. Be comfortable. Sit in a chair, on the floor, or on a cushion. I do not recommend reclining. You may want to use a small rug or cushion set aside for just this purpose. With repeated use, this will create a mind-set in which merely sitting on the rug or cushion triggers the meditative state.

If using a chair, keep your feet flat on the floor, hands in your lap or on your knees in a comfortable position. If sitting on the floor, you may feel comfortable in a yogic position or you may imitate the semi-yogic position as seen in the familiar depiction of the Celtic Horned God, Cernunnos, on the Gundestrup cauldron. Close your eyes and relax, let the tensions of the day drain from your body and drip from your hands. Begin the breathing exercise (inhale to the mental count of two, hold for one count, exhale for two counts). Let the clutter of daily thoughts clear away—dismiss all the little thoughts that seek to intrude and distract you. This is called mind chatter, and goes away if you do not focus on it. Once this is past, you are ready to open your subconscious mind and access the universe. Do not be surprised back into conscious mind dominance simply because you see your surroundings change—this is not unusual.

When you are in a restful state, you can focus on a word or on a question you need answered. If using a guided meditation, record it first, then play it once you feel serene, and let your mind see the images being described so you can feel yourself involved. Visualizations help you to enter an altered state and to comprehend that time, space, and what is considered reality exist only as you perceive them. These then cease to be boundaries, but are unlimited or even nonexistent—as you desire.

After the meditation session ends, take a deep breath and exhale, letting the meditation depart. Take a second deep breath, inhaling the sense of all being right in the world. Exhale and you are back in your meditation place. Ground yourself by touching the floor with the palms of your hands and letting the residual energy drain out. Then have something to eat and drink. This latter activity is the typical grounding practice of Cakes and Wine in Craft rituals. Now you are ready to move on to some routine task. You may want to keep a journal of your meditations to track your development.

Ritual Meditation

Another way to meditate, as demonstrated in the meditation at the end of Chapter 1, is with a ritual setting. This means that a circle is drawn, the Elementals are called on, a candle is lit, incense is burning, and the act of meditating is directed at a magical purpose. You may mark off your circle with stones, candles, or any other objects that help you to focus. You may want to keep a specific set of items to delineate the ritual meditation circle, and possibly represent the Elementals—a shell, nut, stone, feather, lava chunk, or a fired-clay brick are all items that can be used.

The purpose of the ritual determines the color of the candle used and the scent of the incense. You may want to drum or shake a rattle to free your mind and provide a focal point. When the meditation is over, extinguish the candle, farewell the Elementals, and open the circle. This type of meditation is a technique of magical practice in which the desired reality is envisioned so that the manner of bringing it into being is discovered.

Meditation and the Craft

Through your meditations you will come to recognize that all things are interconnected in the same existence. Thus, you want to *be careful in what you do* because *what you send comes back* in one form or another simply because we are all connected. This is where creativity comes in. The primary way to use the dark powers is with a reverse methodology that brings balance and wholeness. You are basically drawing in the dark energy already around you, and redirecting this very powerful energy.

When you find yourself in a situation where you have accumulated negative energy around you, take a moment to meditate. Formulate a question or word key that you will use once you are in the meditative state. I like the question approach best of all. You can ask why this energy is around you; where did it come from; what drew this energy; and what is it that you really want? These are all good questions for determining your reaction to the negativity around you.

With reflection, you come to understand what it is that triggers negative energy within you. It is usually not what you first imagine. While you might think you are angry at someone for what was said or done, actually your anger stems from other sources. It is when you start to examine your reactions that you find what really drew that dark power to you. This power is like a friend, though, not something that you need to fear. It comes to you, drawn by your negative reaction to something, and awaits your directions. This is the universe at its most cleansing and comforting. It is easy to feel comforted when you are in a positive mood, but it takes a special kind of understanding to appreciate the possibilities of comforting when you are in a negative mood.

Consider now the source of your discomfort. Is it that someone bested you at something or that your pride was injured? Did someone betray you or did you draw away? Next, consider what it is that you truly want. Do you want revenge or do you want a new start? If it is revenge, the dark powers will flow in that direction, following your natural inclination, but for the witch, that power is harnessed to work for a more beneficial purpose. Anger is easy; defining the cause within yourself and addressing that is harder.

Once you have determined the cause for the negative energy you feel, you are able to utilize the dark power that is drawn to you by that negativity to transform and release the negative energy. One method is to use this power for something, not against it. In the case I know of where a woman sought to get her husband back from his new girlfriend, she directed her anger energy not at revenge on the woman, but at happiness for the woman with another man. Thus she gave her husband the chance to remember that his wife and children still wanted him.

When you direct the power of negative energy to bring good things to someone you may feel has wronged you, you deflect negative karma while gaining your goal. The meditation process is where you challenge yourself to find the root of your negative energy, and when you sift the cosmos for a solution that is beneficial to all. When you transform your negative energies into a positive focus, you are finally able to release that negativity. The moment the negativity is sent away from you, positive energy slips in to fill the vacancy. The pulsing and switching of polarities exists in the magnetic poles of the earth, and in the energy fields of humans. Through meditation, you can gain better control over your energy fluctuations and guide your own destiny, which is the true goal of any practitioner of magic.

An example of how to direct the dark power toward achieving a positive goal follows in the next ritual.

Knowing a Person Meditation

The black mirror can be the focus for a number of meditations using the power of the dark aspect of the Divine. It can help you to focus on identifying the people around you who have an adverse influence on your life. In Green Witchcraft it is believed that once a person's name is known to you, that person holds no power over you. This refers not to a given name that is known by simple recitation, nor is it the Working Name, by which another practitioner of the Craft works magic, but it is the name that defines how a person relates to you. The *knowing name* is personally descriptive. If there is someone in your life who causes you distress whenever he or she is encountered or thought about, you can alleviate the problem by identifying the source of the discomfort. Knowledge is indeed power, and in this case, that power is defensive and protective (see "Meditation" on page 88.)

Dark Power Tools

Black Mirror

In adapting the information gained from meditation to dark power work, certain tools are especially good for focusing. In previous exercises, I have mentioned the black mirror. This tool is excellent for dark aspect meditations. The blackness of the reflection opens the way to other worlds and realms with ease. A black mirror may be placed on a stand to sit upright so the witch may gaze into the mirror, or the mirror may be held in the hands. Practicality and comfort are the determining factors for the method chosen.

When doing a Companion Quest, it is best to set the mirror in a stand so your hands are free to do other things. With a spell, again, you need freedom of movement and the use of your hands. But if you are doing a journey, you may feel more comfortable sitting in your meditation place with the mirror laying in your hands so that you are looking down into your lap at the mirror.

Gourd Rattle

I like to get a number of colorful gourds for decorations at Samhain. These are readily available at supermarkets and grocery stores during the Halloween and Thanksgiving Day seasons. The natural gourds can be set in a dry place when no longer being used as a decoration. After a few months they dry out and can be turned into a dark power tool. One of my favorites is a small crook neck with a rounded base that fits neatly into the palm of my hand. The natural drying process loosens the seeds, and when the gourd is shaken, the seeds rattle with a smooth swish. Another gourd I like to use is a larger, brightly colored crook neck, with bumps and knobs all over it.

Once you select the gourd you want to keep as a rattle, tell it that you want it to dry out for your use in ritual and meditation. This alerts the energy field around it, the fairy of the gourd, to your desire. Every time you see the gourd, think about it as dried and working as a rattle in your hands. As an experiment, I once selected only one gourd out of a bowl of gourds to be my tool. Sure enough, all the other gourds deteriorated after a few weeks, but not the one I had identified and spoke to as my future tool.

The enthusiasm of your conversation makes a difference, too. Contrary to popular opinion, it is perfectly okay to talk to your vegetables. The ability of the witch to communicate with nature and the objects of nature is one of those things that has bred suspicion about the Craft, but you simply have to keep an open mind about it.

Once the gourd is thoroughly dry (it may take several months), you can inscribe it with symbols that have meaning to you. If you do not want a dried gourd rattle, there are papier-maché gourds that are very charming and easy to work with. The papier-maché ones are typically found in hobby-craft stores or the craft sections of large variety stores. Cowrie shells may be found in shell stores and well-stocked arts and crafts stores, and make an excellent addition to the exterior of the gourd. The seeds that go into a gourd to make the rattle could be no more than the gourd's own seeds dried up inside and shaken loose, seeds selected from the plants of an herb garden, or a combination.

Seeds may be added to a gourd through a small hole made with the point of the athame (a witch's ritual knife) or other sharp object (such as an ice pick) toward the top of the gourd, so that nothing will spill out when the gourd is shaken. In the Old Religion, the magic knife was also the knife used for daily chores. The terms kitchen witch, hedge witch, and cottage witch refer to witches who are in close contact with their magical tools on a daily basis, as part of living. These witches practice witchcraft by incorporating it into their everyday lives and environment.

The visualizations and connections between what is done and what is used with the dark powers come from the realm of the individual's subconscious. An icepick to drill the hole, for example, can be thought of as relating to the Ice Maiden or Snow Queen, or to the icy darkness of deep caverns imagined as an Underworld entrance, the realm of the Dark Lord and the Cailleach (Crone).

The hole may be left open or sealed with wax or a bit of cork whittled to fit. Leaving the hole open in the gourd may symbolize the accessibility of the Underworld, a "spirit hole" as it were, while sealing it with wax may symbolize containment of the promise (seeds) of regeneration within the womb (gourd) of the Dark Goddess.

Cowrie shells are symbolic of the Goddess and fertility, and as such they may be strung together to form a net of shells that may then be attached around the lower portion of the exterior of the gourd. These add to the rattle and as vulvic symbols represent the passage to rebirth.

Because the gourd is used in dark aspect and Otherworld connection, and loud or abrasive sounds are not generated within the Goddess womb, the harsher noises of pebbles or dried beans are not as suitable as the quieter tones of smaller herbal seeds. Dill, fennel, hyssop, all herbs of protection, coriander, symbolic of the Divine Within, and poppy seed, symbolic of the Underworld, provide excellent seed additions for the gourd.

The exterior of the gourd may be carved or painted with ogham, runes, or Craft symbols, the name of the practitioner, and designs of the dark aspect of the Divine. Traditional ancient designs used for the god, the goddess, death, and rebirth include spirals, chevrons, triangles, equal-armed crosses, swastikas, snakes, curving horns, the double axe, butterflies, and lozenges.

Ogham

Celtic Ogham markings, which relate to trees and associations through those trees may be related to the dark powers in a variety of interpretations. The Ogham is more fully discussed in Chapter 6, but for now, the dark-oriented Ogham symbols could include:

Beth	⊤	Birch (for the Winter Goddess)
Luis	⊤⊤	Rowan (for protective magics)
Nion	⊤⊤⊤	Ash (for connection to the Worlds—World Tree)
Duir	⊥	Oak (for the Doorway to the Inner Realms)
Tinne	⊥⊥⊥	Holly (for the Winter God)
Coll	⊥⊥⊥⊥	Hazel (for Witchcraft)
Quert	⊥⊥⊥⊥⊥	Apple (for the Otherworld)
Muin	⟋	Vine (for libation wine)
Gort	⟋⟋	Ivy (for the Underworld)
Ngetal	⟋⟋⟋	Cranberry/Guelder Rose (for the Dark Lord)
Straif	⟋⟋⟋⟋	Blackthorn (for the Dark Lady)
Ruis	⟋⟋⟋⟋⟋	Elder (for the Crone)
Ailim	+	Pine (for hidden knowledge)
Eadha	⧺⧺	Aspen (for passage to the Otherworld)
Iodho	⧺⧺⧺	Yew (for passage to the Underworld)

Runes

Runic symbols that could be used to decorate the gourd include:

Thorn	Þ	Giant (for protection)
As	ᚠ	The God (for wisdom)
Rad	ᚱ	Wheel (for path to what is sought)
Ken	ᚲ	Wood (for light to guide the Spirit)
Haegal	ᚺ	Hail (for Shadows)
Is	ᛁ	Ice (for secretiveness/Ice World)
Eoh	ᛇ	Yew (for passage to new life/rebirth)
Elhaz	ᛉ	Elk (for the Horned God)
Tyr	↑	Arrow (for victory)
Beorc	ᛒ	Birch (for the Goddess)
Eh	ᛗ	Horse (for trust and a guide in the Otherworld)
Lagu	ᛚ	Water (for psychic growth and intuition)
Odal	ᛟ	Earth (for the Underworld)
Daeg	ᛞ	Dawn/Dusk (for working between the Worlds)

Dark Power Colors

The following colors are best suited for dark power rituals and spells. These colors are used in candles, altar coverings, decorations, and spellworking materials to invoke the energy of the dark powers.

Black: absorb/block negativity; focus on discord; remove negativity; focus on Underworld (or Shadowland); Crone/Dark Lord visualizations; utilize energy of the Wild Hunt

Gray: Fairy paths; working with the Sidhe; focus on Otherworld; neutralizing negativity; cancellation of negativity; veiling work; focus on stalemate

Purple: spiritual development; spiritual power; spiritual cleansing; enhancing intuition; tension release; progress; confronting disease

White: protection; truth; meditation; peace; sincerity; purity; removing doubts; overcoming fears; overcoming problems; mental and emotional cleansing

Red: power; enthusiasm; energy; strength; vigor; love; control over own destiny; thwart the control of others over you; courage

Lavender: Sidhe magics; spiritual development; psychic growth; divination; sensitivity; blessings

Silver: lunar energy

Ritual Timing

As a tool of the Craft, a cleansing and dedicating ritual such as given in the Dark Moon Ritual at the end of Chapter 2 will empower the gourd for use in dark aspect rituals and meditations.

For a dark aspect tool intended for use in dark rituals, Otherworld travel, Shadowland communication, and dark power meditations, the best time to do a consecration ritual that incorporates the features of cleansing and dedication is during a Dark Moon Esbat, particularly in October for proximity to Samhain, or the other dark months of September and November. Spell magic is not normally performed during the Dark Moon because the mythology suggests that the god is withdrawn into the goddess in her tomb/womb aspect.

Esbats for the New Moon are typically the time for banishment magics (getting rid of bad habits, poverty, loneliness, and so forth) and are performed on the first day of the New Moon, when there is the thinnest sliver of light showing. Magic work is acceptable during the Dark Moon, however, when consecrating a dark aspect tool, because the very element of the mystery of that transforming instant from Tomb to Womb is being called upon. The Sidhe Moon offers another opportunity for Dark Aspect empowerment of a tool, and the Sidhe may be called upon for a consecration at this time. The practitioner has to determine what feels comfortable for timing.

In the cave of the Oracle of Delphi, the tripod in its place, faint swirls of steam seeping from the fissure, the chamber wrapped in expectant silence—the Oracle is waiting to speak and to be heard again. The symbol of Her wisdom is the Python.

— Meditation —
Meditation of Knowing

You may want to insert the following meditation into a Dark Moon Esbat, or simply create a circle and call upon the Elementals to guard the sacred space, using the imagery from the Dark Moon Esbat. Have at hand a black candle (may be votive, pillar, or stick), a black mirror, incense, and a drum or gourd rattle. Be seated either before the altar where this is done or at a table used for this meditation. Light the black candle in its holder and say:

This candle glows to light the path into darkness.

Place the candle in front of the mirror and light an incense that appeals to you as a night scent. Place it in front of the candle. Drum or shake a gourd rattle against the palm of your hand as you chant:

I seek the name of one who bids me ill;
Whose heart toward me is malice filled.
No chastisement do I make,
But free myself for my own sake.

Chant until you are looking beyond the image in the mirror. Let the candlelight and incense work to help words come into your mind that describe the feelings that person causes in yourself (there could be quite a few). Now look into the person with your mind's eye and let words come that describe the person.

Images of the person may now start to come into focus in the mirror. Each image will have some characteristic that is the same, and this is the point of recognition of what defines that person in relation to yourself. Find the words that match your feelings with the dominant characteristic of the person; try several combinations until you have a name that defines the person and focuses on your awareness of that person.

Now you know, or ken, who the person is, and you can feel the peace and serenity of that knowledge; that person will no longer be able to raise emotional distress in you because you know that person's name.

To clear the mirror, lift the incense before the mirror and blow air across the burner so the smoke is blown into the mirror, and say:

> *The image is seen, the name is known,*
> *No more do I need this view in my home.*
> *Swirl the smoke of incense tonight,*
> *Banish the image of* (descriptive name) *from my sight!*

Snuff the black candle and cover the mirror with a black cloth. You may now proceed with the Esbat ritual; or bless and farewell the Elementals, open the circle, take some refreshment, and move back into a normal routine.

— Herbal Meditation —
The Oracle Cave

There are a variety of dark aspect meditations, and many of those used in the practice of Green Witchcraft open the subconscious awareness through the use of burning herbs. A favorite herb for this use is mugwort, but other choices could include sage, lemon grass, burdock, woodruff, and rosemary. The purpose of the following meditation is to reconnect with our pagan past through the Oracle Cave.

When the famous Oracle of Delphi cave was closed, a curious thing occurred. The entrance to the cavern was sealed, and to this day, of all the temple ruins, people are only forbidden from standing over the entrance to the Oracle. At night, the place is illuminated and there is a guard posted. In the underground chamber of the Oracle, there is said to be a split in the rock from which escape the vapors of prophecies. In ancient times and through the early centuries of Christianity, a priestess sat on a tripod over the crack, inhaled the vapors, and uttered her prophecies.

It is easy to imagine the tripod in its place, faint swirls of steam seeping from the fissure, the chamber wrapped in expectant silence—the Oracle waiting to speak and to be heard again. The site was sacred to the Goddess for at least three thousand years. The symbol of Her wisdom was the Python, which the much more recent Hellenic mythology claimed was slain by Apollo. The temple did transfer hands from the priestesses of the ancient Great Goddess to the priesthood of Apollo with the conquest of Greece by the Hellenes, but even then, only a priestess could act as a channel between the worlds. With this background information, you may begin the meditation, so that you may feel yourself approach and enter this dark, stone chamber.

In a cauldron, light either an incense charcoal disk (these can be purchased in rolls at most shops that sell incense) or a black votive candle. Have a bundle of the desired herbs, such as mugwort, handy, along with your knife and your wand. Using the knife, create your Circle and sacred space. With your wand, call upon the Elementals, whose candles at the Quarters should be purple. Sit on the floor (or at a table in the center of the Circle you have created) so that the cauldron is in front of you. Add mugwort (or other herb of your choice) to the candle (or charcoal) and watch it smolder.

You may want to drum or use a gourd rattle as you let your thoughts move you back in time and memory. Watch the smoke as it swirls, adding herbs as needed, and focus on the smoke. See it as a gray mist that seems to part around you and envelope you, moving you through the swirls of time so that *now* and *then* are one. You remember and you experience on both levels of time converged within you, and now you are in modern Greece, visiting historic ruins; the fumes of the old-fashioned bus come to you, and the dust stirred by the old tires on the dirt road as the bus rolls to a stop at the site of the ancient Oracle of Delphi.

You have hidden a small flashlight in your pocket for this occasion, and have arrived with a busload of tourists. You moved around the dry, sun-baked temple sites and ruins of columns while listening in a distracted way to the prepared speech of the guide. All the while, you have been waiting for your chance to explore the forbidden spot, and now the tour guide moves on with the other visitors. You see the gap at the corner of the stone slab, and feel a rush of cool air, and you know that this is the way in. The monotonous voice of the guide fades, you quickly push aside the loose broken stones near the gap of the slab, and you find the step beneath allows you room to squeeze inside.

How Are the Dark Powers Used?

At first there is only darkness and a distant sound hard to describe. Your first thought is that there might be snakes inside, but then you relax as you realize that you are in a sacred place, not as an intruder, but as one who is part of this tradition. No snake will attack you here—if any are in this place, they will feel your peace and ignore you. The heat of the surface world vanishes and is replaced by the coolness of the subterranean Earth. You move down the steps and the darkness becomes a gloom through which you can barely see, but it is not impenetrable. Your light shows the winding stairway is uninhabited—perhaps there are volcanic gases that keep animals away. You hear a distant sound and wonder if you could be in danger of succumbing to some poisonous gas, but there is a breeze drifting through the chamber and out the gap where you entered, so the air is breathable and not at all stifling.

The steps take you down further and the sound suddenly makes sense to you—it is the hissing of the vapors escaping the fissure. You have reached the bottom of the stairway now, and the floor is uneven but smooth. You realize that it is bedrock. Carefully, you make your way across the chamber toward the hissing sound, and then you see a thin crack in the floor. As you scan across the floor with your flashlight, you see that the crack widens slightly, and you move along the side of the crack to see where it will lead you. And then something glints in the light. Your breath is caught in your throat and your eyes smart with tears—you are seeing the brass tripod, still standing where it was last used, waiting for a priestess to ascend and sit on it.

You set the flashlight on the floor and make the sign of the pentacle in the air before you, then you move toward the seat of wisdom, stepping across the fissure in the process. You touch the tripod and feel a tremor of excitement as you realize that no one has touched this seat in over a thousand years. You know where you belong, and you take your place on the tripod.

Now you hear a sound, then more sounds, a babble of sounds: "Areth; amoad; aneadi; careth; imionee; trianeth . . ."

The words come faster and stronger and louder, and you begin to recognize their meanings and that there are visions attached to these words, and you suddenly realize that the sounds are pouring from *your* mouth! Tears flow down your cheeks and you know that the Goddess is speaking and you are Her Priestess. The cavern is filled with your speech and ecstasy. You hear what She tells you and what She reveals to you, and you know that the Goddess lives—through all vain human denial, the Lady *lives* and *is life*, and *gives life!*

Slowly the sounds begin to fade, and you become aware of a chill. You are soaked in perspiration, but the presence of the Goddess now feels warm around you, and you feel you are wrapped in Her cloak. You are calmer now, and saddened as you realize that this sacred place is closed off to the people who want to come here. She comforts you and you hear Her voice tell you: "I am in all places of the Earth and in your heart. Take this tripod into your heart and sit on it whenever you have need to speak with Me, for I am everywhere."

You understand now that the whole of the Earth is Her temple and that anywhere you are when you call upon Her is the same as sitting upon the tripod in this cavern to hear Her voice. Your connection with Her is complete, and the Oracle now resides within.

You have the courage now to slip off the stool and cross the fissure back to your flashlight. You scan the walls and see the beautiful carvings and the great python carved around the rock of the fissure.

You take a deep breath and release it, then turn away from the tripod and walk back to the steps as though you had done it a hundred times—perhaps once you had. You ascend the stairway and return to the outer world. You were not missed; you hear the voice of the guide coming back your way, and you quickly re-set the stone in place and leave the forbidden spot. Now you are protective of this sacred site and in a moment of anxiety, you fear what might happen if others learn of your experience; who knows what damage they might do to prevent others from entering. Then you smile and realize—of course, others have entered before you; others who are your kindred; and you feel warmed inside as you understand that you are not alone.

You breathe deeply and exhale. The voices of the crowd dissipate. Breathe again, and you are returned to your meditation circle. Have something to eat and drink, let the incense die out, put away your tools, and return to a normal routine.

By entering into the Oracle Cave, you connect with the tradition of the priestesses of the Goddess from multiple millennia past into the present. That the cave is sealed is no longer important, for the cave has been opened by the mind and the spirit. The physical limits imposed by a hostile religion have been transcended and made intuitive, only to have the intuitive in turn manifested through the energy of the Practitioner of the Craft. The Age of Aquarius is the manifestation of the power of psychic energy, and the more people who embark upon these types of meditations and visualizations, the stronger the manifesting power. In time, the Oracle will be re-opened, and a priestess will again be seated upon the sturdy, ancient tripod, and the voice of the Goddess will be heard by all who come to Her sacred place.

6

How Is the Celtic Ogham
Used in Divination?

Envisioning the Ogham

There are many ways to connect with the light and dark powers through meditation and divination. The wisdom of the Crone and the hidden knowledge of the Dark Lord may be found in the tarot, a crystal ball, a black mirror, runes, and the ogham.

An ancient motif that Joseph Campbell (*The Masks of God: Primitive Mythology*, Penguin Books, 1976) describes as "the queens and their king" is seen in early Sumeria, later Mycenea, and in the Celtic ogham tradition with the realms of each world of the Celtic cosmology ruled, or influenced, by one of the Three Queens or their

King. The realms are arranged in Quarters, aspected to the Queens of the North, West, and East, and the King of the South. To visualize this, think of three large squares, then imagine two lines to quarter each square as an "X". On each square, then, the top space between the lines is North, the bottom space is South, the left space is West, and the right space is East.

Otherworld   Middleworld   Underworld

Each realm in each world, and the four paths between the worlds, corresponds to an ogham few. The paths traverse through the point where the lines of the "X" intersect, called the *fifths*. The path fews connect the three squares for a three-dimensional reading.

Otherworld: N = Age — Iodha (I)

W = Light — Quert (Q)

E = Abundance — Ruis (R)

S = Happiness — Nion (N)

PATHS: 1 = Eadha (E)

2 = Coll (C)

3 = Straif (Z)

4 = Saille (S)

Middleworld: N = Challenge — Ur (U)

W = Knowledge — Tinne (T)

E = Prosperity — Ngetal (Ng)

S = Contentment — Fearn (F)

PATHS: 1 = Onn (O)

2 = Duir (D)

3 = Gort (G)

4 = Luis (L)

Underworld: N = Endings — Ailm (A)   †

W = Love — Huath (H)   ⊥⊥

E = Growth — Muin (M)   ⫻

S = Energy — Beithe (B)   ⊤

The blank few is seen as cosmic influence, destiny, or fate in the area in which it lands. The quarter read for the blank is determined by whether or not there are path fews in that quarter.

Creating a Casting Cloth

To use the ogham for divination and meditation, create a *casting cloth* symbolizing Middleworld, by cutting out a large square, then sew or draw the large "X" on the square. Draw or sew a smaller square near the center of the cloth. Draw or sew the symbols of the Three Queens and the King on the line of the inner square that passes through the appropriate quarter:

N = Cath (IO) — Friction — two superimposed X's ⨉

W = Fis (UI) — Enlightenment — a spiral curl ꙩ

E = Blath (AE) — Harvest — a grid ▦

S = Seis (OI) — Balance — two triangles, base to base ⧮

Midhe (EA) — Focal Point — the "X" at the very center of the square

Buy or make a set of ogham fews with a slip of wood inscribed with the symbol of each few as shown here. The casting cloth holds the fews when not in use: place the fews in the center of the cloth, gather up the edges and tie the cloth with a cord so that it forms a bag.

Throwing a Spread

To throw a spread, open the cloth and lay it out flat. Gather the fews into your hands and concentrate on a particular question or information that you want to learn. The ogham respond well to a question format and the meanings of the fews can be brought together for a concise response. Lightly toss the fews into the air over the cloth and watch them land. The ones that fall with the backside up, remove into a pile. The ones that fall outside the cloth, remove to that same pile. Read what is left.

The throw initiates in the Middleworld and departure from this world occurs only with "path" fews. See what quarter has the most fews; this will tell you the major power involved in the reading. Next, see if there are path fews present. They are interpreted in two realms—moving the reading from the the realm (quarter) in which they have fallen into that of the world according to which they provide transit: four fews move to Otherworld, four to Underworld. The paths move in two directions, so if you begin in Middleworld and travel to Underworld, then encounter another path few connecting these two worlds, you are moved from Underworld back to Middleworld.

If there are fews present that represent realms from other worlds without paths present, this shows that there is Otherworld or Underworld influence in the Middleworld quarter of the reading. If path fews are also present, there is a definite passage of energy for the questioner in the matter being investigated. Fews inside the inner square relate strongest to the focus.

On one casting cloth there is the potential for three worlds to be seen during any throw, and interpretations drawn from a pool of 252 placements of fews in worlds and realms. Add to this the combination of fews that can exist in any given throw, and the possibilities for readings are virtually limitless. For convenience, interpretations are listed at the end of this chapter. When you read a throw, guide your interpretation by the question being asked and the other fews/worlds/realms addressed in the throw. You can best draw a conclusion only after all the elements of the reading are compiled. Then try to put this into a coherent reply statement.

How Is the Celtic Ogham Used in Divination?

If only path fews are thrown, then the questioner is searching and gathering experience and knowledge along the paths shown. Things are in motion for this person and the placement of the fews can show how matters are likely to progress. If only realm fews turn up on the cloth, the questioner is not moving between the worlds so much as the worlds are interjecting their influence into the person's life on a matter.

In any interpretation, then, the fews thrown must be considered by the world in which they lie, the realm in which they lie, the paths indicated, and the realms that the paths link together.

Begin the reading with the few(s) closest to the center of the cloth (the focal point: fifth), and read the rest starting to the left of the first few read and moving clockwise in a circle until you are back where you started. The few at the center tells the focus of the reading. When the blank few appears, there is cosmic power, or destiny, involved in the world/realm in which it appears. If it appears at the center, the focus is on a person's destiny.

Overall, the reading uses:

a. The fews to be read

b. The Middleworld casting cloth

c. The Quarters of the casting cloth

d. Paths from the Middleworld to upper and lower worlds

e. Otherworld and Underworld seen on the same casting cloth, but at different levels due to the path fews

The interpretation involves:

a. Reading the fews by their individual meanings

b. Reading the fews by their closeness to the center

c. Reading the fews by the Quarter influence: Cath ✕ , Fis ⟋ , Blath ▦ , and Seis ⬦

d. Reading the fews by the world and realm they are in

e. Reading the fews by the Quarter influence in the world and realm accessed through a path few

The Worlds and Realms

The following is a listing of the worlds: the realms divided by the directional quarters (N = North, W = West, E = East, S = South); their respective qualities; their Celtic names and meanings; their representative fews; the trees and letters of the fews; the symbols of the fews; and the meanings of the fews. The path fews are listed by few, tree, letter, symbol, and meaning.

Using this listing, toss the fews into the air over the casting cloth, remove the ones that are not going to be read, and read the remainder, starting at the centermost and moving left in a circle. Read each few as its meaning in the world and realm in which it resides. A path few is read in the current realm, then again in the realm it travels to, thus removing the continued reading to the world connected by that few until another path few moves the reading elsewhere.

If beginning in Middleworld, for example, and you come to the few, Coll, read the meaning of Coll in that quarter of Middleworld, then in that realm of Otherworld. The next fews continue to be read in the Otherworld realms. If after a couple of fews, you come to Eadha, you read the meaning of that few in the realm of Otherworld in which it lies, and in the realm of Middleworld where it now takes you. The next fews will continue to be read in Middleworld. If you are in Otherworld and come to the few Onn, you read the meaning of that few in the realm of Otherworld in which it resides, and your passage to Underworld takes the reading through the fifth of Middleworld and into the same quarter of Underworld. The reading continues in Underworld until you come to a path few that connects to Middleworld or Otherworld.

Otherworld — Magh Mor

Qtr.	Qualities	Celtic Names	Fews	Meanings
N	Age/Wisdom	Sen Magh Ancient Plain)	Iodha ⋕ (yew/I)	change; transformation; death; immortality
W	Light/Gentleness/Inspiration	Magh Argetnel Silvery Plain	Quert ⊥⊥⊥ (apple/Q)	regeneration; beauty; life; eternity; perfection
E	Abundance	Magh Mell Delightful Plain	Ruis ⫽ (elder/R)	change; evolution; old ways discarded
S	Happiness	Magh Ionganidh Wondrous Plain	Nion ⊤⊤⊤⊤ (ash/N)	awakening; rebirth; peace; new influence; communication

Paths to Otherworld

1. Eadha (aspen/E)   ⋕   = intuition; overcoming obstacles; sensitivity

2. Coll (hazel/C)   ⊥⊥⊥   = wisdom; creativity; perception; understanding; writing/science

3. Straif (blackthorn/ ST, Z)   ⫽   = destructive power that can be turned against obstacles; coercion; control by force

4. Saille (willow/S)   ⊤⊤⊤   = intuition; flexibility; enchantment; psychic power; liberation

Middleworld — Midhe/Bith

Qtr.	Qualities	Celtic Names	Fews	Meanings
N	Conflict/Resistance/Challenge	Cath ✕ (io)	Ur ⋕ (heather/U)	gateway; success; gains; zeal; self-expression
W	Learning/Knowledge	Fis ↶ (ui)	Tinne ⊥⊥⊥ (holly/T)	balance; tests; choices; retribution; decisions;
E	Prosperity/Harvest	Blath ⊞ (ae)	Ngetal ⫽ (reed/NG)	harmony; inner transformation; inner development
S	Harmony/Contentment	Seis ◇ (oi)	Fearn ⊤⊤⊤ (alder/F)	inner strength; foundations; awareness; confidence
M	Central Focus:	Midhe (–) ✕	Blank — (mistletoe)	cosmic forces

Paths to Underworld

1. Onn (gorse/O) ‖ = opportunity; wisdom gathered; life changes

2. Duir (oak/D) ⊥⊥ = truth; endurance; strength; willpower; able to overcome obstacles

3. Gort (ivy/G) ∥ = tenacity; persistence gains goals; learning; developing skills

4. Luis (rowan/L) ℼ = insight; foreknowledge; cleansing; healing; enhanced creativity

Underworld — Tir Andomain

Qtr.	Qualities	Celtic Names	Fews	Meanings
N	Endings/ Transformation	Tir feThruinn Land Under the Waves	Ailm † (fir/A)	vigor; discretion; secrecy; rulership
W	Love	Tir na Ban Land of the Lady	Huath ⊥ (hawthorn/H)	joy; positive changes; cleansing
E	Growth	Tir na N'og Land of Youth	Muin ⁄ (vine/M)	other sight; reflection; introspection; fruition
S	Vitality/ Energy	Tir na Beo Land of Life	Beithe T (birch/B)	beginnings; energy; unseen forces of growth working

Path/Realm and Few Location

In the chart that follows (page 103), the realms and paths are represented as follows: Otherworld (O), Middleworld (M), and Underworld (U).

List of Ogham Fews

Few Name	Few	Letter	Path/Realm	Few Interpretation
Beithe (Birch)	⊤	B	Realm (U)	Beginnings/Energy
Luis (Rowan)	⊤⊤	L	Path (U)	Insight/Foreknowledge/Enlivening
Fearn (Alder)	⊤⊤⊤	F	Realm (M)	Inner Strength/Foundations
Saille (Willow)	⊤⊤⊤⊤	S	Path (O)	Intuition/Flexibility
Nion (Ash)	⊤⊤⊤⊤⊤	N	Realm (O)	Awakening/Rebirth/Peace
Huath (Hawthorn)	⊥	H	Realm (U)	Pleasure/Misfortune/Cleansing
Duir (Oak)	⊥⊥	D	Path (U)	Truth/Endurance/Strength
Tinne (Holly)	⊥⊥⊥	T	Realm (M)	Balance/Retribution
Coll (Hazel)	⊥⊥⊥⊥	C	Path (O)	Wisdom/Creativity/Perception
Quert (Apple)	⊥⊥⊥⊥⊥	Q	Realm (O)	Regeneration/Eternity/Life
Muin (Vine)	⟋	M	Realm (U)	Introspection/Other Sight
Gort (Ivy)	⫽	G	Path (U)	Developing Skills/Learning
Ngetal (Reed)	⫻	NG	Realm (M)	Harmony/Inner Development
Straif (Blackthorn)	⫽⫽	Z	Path (O)	Coercion/Control Through Force
Ruis (Elder)	⫽⫽⫽	R	Realm (O)	Change/Evolution
Ailm (Fir)	†	A	Realm (U)	Rulership/Vigor/Discretion
Onn (Gorse)	‡	O	Path (U)	Wisdom Collated /Life Changes
Ur (Heather)	⧻	U	Realm (M)	Fervor/Gateway/Success/Gains
Eadha (Aspen)	⧻⧻	E	Path (O)	Intuition/Overcoming Obstacles
Iodho (Yew)	⧻⧻⧻	I/Y	Realm (O)	Transformation/Ends/Immortality
Blank (Mistletoe)	—	Blank	None	Cosmic Influence/Destiny/Fate

A Complete Listing for Ogham Interpretation

In the following list of 252 interpretations for the ogham fews, each few meaning is given with the placement in which the few could fall in a throw. The few is first, then the World abbreviated as OW (Otherworld), MW (Middleworld), and UW (Underworld). Next is the quarter of that world in which the few could fall, abbreviated as N (North), W (West), E (East), and S (South). As ever in divination, the intuition of the reader comes into play for the nuances and connections between the fews, worlds, realms, and the questioner.

1. ▦ Transformation/Ends/Immortality

Iodha in the following placements:

OW-N: Age or wisdom brings an ending, transformation, immortality

OW-W: Changed by light of inspiration or by gentleness

OW-E: Ending of bounty or transformation into abundance

OW-S: Ending of one kind of happiness; change in joy

MW-N: Challenge motivates a change; brings immortality

MW-W: Transformed by new knowledge

MW-E: Reaping a small harvest; change in prosperity

MW-S: Contentment/harmony ends and interests change

UW-N: Period of significant endings and changes

UW-W: Transformation of love to immortality; end of a love

UW-E: Youthfulness transformed by growth

UW-S: Life changes; end of one kind of life is transformed with new Energy into another; new vitality

2. ▥ Regeneration/Eternity/Life

Quert in the following placements:

OW-N: Age or wisdom brings a regeneration or a new Life

OW-W: New calmness in life; perfection in peacefulness

OW-E: Renewal of abundance

OW-S: Happiness from a new life; enjoyment of beauty

MW-N: Challenge leads to regeneration or a new life

MW-W: Renewal/perfecting of knowledge

MW-E: Return of prosperity; upturn in fortune; reap rewards
MW-S: Contentment from beauty/perfection; harmony in life
UW-N: Ending brings regeneration; perfection ideal changes
UW-W: Love renewed; love of life, beauty, the arts
UW-E: Growth brings new youthfulness; eternally young
UW-S: Energy and life revitalized

3. ⵗ Change/Evolution

Ruis in the following placements:
OW-N: Wisdom leads to new path; old ways decay; evolution into new forms
OW-W: Lack of contentment inspires search for a new path; peace comes from releasing what is outmoded
OW-E: Change in bounty; deterioration of delight pushes for new path
OW-S: Old forms of happiness replaced with new ones
MW-N: Challenge to old ways leads to new forms
MW-W: Learning brings changes; knowledge results in evolution
MW-E: Gains deteriorate/not as great as expected; new methods needed for success
MW-S: Contentment/harmony comes in due course; that which brings satisfaction is in a state of change; seeking new goals
UW-N: Old patterns give way to new ideas; need to adjust to changes
UW-W: New love coming; seeking new friends
UW-E: Evolution and growth emphasized to maintain youthful outlook
UW-S: Old ways revitalized to produce a new perspective; change through energy

4. ⵑ Awakening/Rebirth/Peace

Nion in the following placements:
OW-N: Awakening and communication of wisdom; new influence through age/longevity/tenure
OW-W: Peace emphasized; inspiration and rebirth; hope
OW-E: Abundance brings peace; fruitful communications; reward
OW-S: Happiness communicated; new joy in life

MW-N: Challenges open awareness; friction soothed by communication and influence; renewal of efforts

MW-W: New awareness through learning; communication of knowledge; old knowledge reborn

MW-E: Prosperity through communication; peaceful harvest

MW-S: New influence leads to harmony/contentment; awakening to the things that matter

UW-N: Awakening and rebirth changes endings to new beginnings and brings transformations into being

UW-W: Love/pleasure re-discovered; peace in relationships through communication; love as a new influence

UW-E: Rebirth of youth; awakening of growing process; communication/new influence with youth

UW-S: revitalization; re-energized; vital communications; dynamic renewal of efforts

5. ▥ Intuition/Overcoming Obstacles—Path to Otherworld

Eadha in the following placements:

OW-N: Sensitive to elders; wisdom gained through intuition

OW-W: Inspiration by intuition; peace gained through perseverance

OW-E: Obstacles overcome to gain abundance; willing sharing of bounty

OW-S: Kindliness leads to happiness; follow instincts for bliss

MW-N: Challenges overcome; intuition is accurate

MW-W: Knowledge comes intuitively; obstacles to learning overcome; sensitive use of knowledge

MW-E: Obstacles overcome to gain prosperity; rewards from caring for others

MW-S: Intuition/sensitivity leads to harmony/contentment; obstacles to harmony overcome

UW-N: Transformed by intuition; obstacles end

UW-W: Sensitivity to others increases love and pleasure; follow intuition in matters of the heart

UW-E: Enjoyment of youth; intuition leads to growth

UW-S: Energy to overcome obstacles; strong intuition

6. ⅢⅢ Wisdom/Creativity/Perception—Path to Otherworld

Coll in the following placements:

OW-N: Strong wisdom; career in science/writing/creativity; mental power; understanding is accurate

OW-W: Inspirational turn of mind; spiritual writing; perceptions for peacefulness

OW-E: Bounty and abundance from wisdom and creative expression

OW-S: Understanding brings happiness; joy in writing/science

MW-N: Wisdom/understanding challenged; friction in creativity

MW-W: Educational writing; perceptive ability increases knowledge; participation in learning

MW-E: Prosperity from creativity/understanding

MW-S: Wisdom leads to harmony; contentment from creativity

UW-N: Transformation of wisdom; misunderstanding; perceptions change

UW-W: Love of learning; pleasure in creative efforts

UW-E: Wisdom grows; youthful audience; writing for young people; science endeavors beginning to grow; creativity and understanding increases

UW-S: Energy to pursue interests

7. ⫻ Coercion/Control Through Force—Path to Otherworld

Straif in the following placements:

OW-N: Wisdom controlled by others; obstacles of age turned to benefits

OW-W: Inspiration muted; peace enforced by others; dissatisfaction

OW-E: Abundance lacking; bounty dissipated

OW-S: Happiness muted by others; own joy lies in the hands of others

MW-N: Challenged to seize control of own life; use destructive power against obstacles

MW-W: Learning is a difficult process; knowledge seems controlled and constricted; need to explore new ideas

MW-E: Prosperity controlled by others; obstacles to goals need to be overcome for independence and success

MW-S: Disharmony; discontent; need to break free of constraints to attain own contentment

UW-N: Destructive power turned against obstacles; ending of coercion; transformation of negative forces into positive ones

UW-W: Forbearance in love; false pleasure; pretense of love; dominance in love can lead to its destruction; resignation to will of others in love/pleasure

UW-E: Growth inhibited; control of youth

UW-S: Energy controlled by others; vitality dependent on others

8. ᛏ Intuition/Flexibility—Path to Otherworld

Saille in the following placements:

OW-N: Wisdom enhanced by psychic power; liberation in age

OW-W: Flexibility for peace; intuition leads to inspiration

OW-E: Abundance gives liberation; bounty through intuition

OW-S: Happiness comes from flexibility; intuition/psychic power brings bliss

MW-N: Challenge to use psychic power wisely; friction eased by flexibility

MW-W: Flexibility in learning and knowledge; wide variety of interests; intuitive learning; liberation through knowledge

MW-E: Prosperity from intuition and psychic power; what is sent comes back

MW-S: Use of intuition to find contentment; in harmony with power; contentment from adaptability

UW-N: Psychic power is transforming; end of restrictions

UW-W: Love is intuitive; adaptability in finding love and enjoyment; liberation in love; psychic power enhances love

UW-E: Growth of intuition and psychic power

UW-S: Psychic energy; vitality of freedom; keenly intuitive

9. ᚻ Fervor/Gateway/Success/Gains

Ur in the following placements:

OW-N: Wisdom provides a gateway to strong self-expression/gains

OW-W: Inspirational fervor; peace from success

OW-E: Success brings abundance

OW-S: Happiness through strong self-expression; gains bring bliss

MW-N: Friction leads to strong self-expression; challenge brings success

108

MW-W: Gains in knowledge/learning; self-expression in knowledge; philosopher; education is a gateway to success

MW-E: Highly successful; many gains; fervor and self-expression reap successful harvest

MW-S: Harmony from successes; strong self-expression harmonized for contentment and gains

UW-N: Self-expression is a gateway to transformation; gains dwindle and new forms for success need to be found

UW-W: Enjoyment of self-expression; pleasure from success; ardent in pursuit of love and pleasure

UW-E: Success is a gateway to growth; youthful self-expression

UW-S: Energy and fervor invigorate self-expression and gains

10. ⃛ Balance/Retribution

Tinne in the following placements:

OW-N: Age and wisdom bring new challenges for balance

OW-W: Peace through balance

OW-E: Balance needed in decisions affecting bounty

OW-S: Choices to be made for happiness

MW-N: Challenges to balance mounting; retribution/justice; care needed in making decisions in time of friction

MW-W: Learning determined by conscious decisions; balanced education; tests of knowledge

MW-E: Balance needed for prosperity; choices determine the harvest

MW-S: Contentment from balance; harmony affected by decisions

UW-N: Endings from retribution; transformation to balance by decisions

UW-W: Balance in love and pleasure; love a matter of decisions rather than emotion; pleasure/love test balance; retribution in love

UW-E: Balanced growth; tests in youth; decisions/choices affect growth

UW-S: Energy to maintain balance; vitality to overcome tests; choices approached with vigor

11. ⚡ Harmony/Inner Development

Ngetal in the following placements:

OW-N: Age/wisdom brings internal transformation/development

OW-W: Harmony from inspiration; peacefulness within

OW-E: Abundance comes from inner development

OW-S: Happiness lies in internal transformation

MW-N: Harmony difficult to maintain; inner development challenged; friction leads to internal transformation

MW-W: Knowledge/learning has a profound, transformative affect

MW-E: Balance is harvest of inner development

MW-S: Harmony/contentment emphasized through internal transformation

UW-N: Transformation emphasized through internal development and harmony; end of harmony through internal transformation

UW-W: Internal transformation/inner development through love; harmony in pleasure

UW-E: Growth of harmony; youthful inner transformation; emphasis on inner development

UW-S: Energy for internal transformation/development; vitality for harmony

12. ᛏ Inner Strength/Foundations

Fearn in the following placements:

OW-N: Wisdom emphasized as awareness ends doubts; inner strength through wisdom/age

OW-W: Inspiration to inner strength; peace through end of doubt

OW-E: Foundation of abundance; awareness/appreciation of bounty; generosity

OW-S: Foundation of happiness; bliss from awareness/end of doubts; satisfaction

MW-N: Friction leads to ending of doubts; challenge brings inner strength

MW-W: Learning ends doubts; foundation of knowledge brings inner strength

MW-E: Prosperity from determination

MW-S: Contentment from awareness and end of doubts; harmony from inner strength

UW-N: Awareness is transformative; ending of doubts emphasized; inner strength develops

UW-W: Love faced with full awareness; inner strength brings pleasure; doubt-free love

UW-E: Growth of awareness to overcome doubts; youthful foundation of inner strength

UW-S: Vitality of inner strength; energy to open awareness

13. ⊦ Wisdom Collated/Life Changes—Path to Underworld

Onn in the following placements:

OW-N: Wisdom emphasized through opportunity; life changes due to age/wisdom gathered

OW-W: Positive changes from gathered wisdom lead to peace; inspiration generates life changes

OW-E: Opportunity for abundance; bountiful wisdom

OW-S: Happiness from opportunity and wisdom applied to create life changes

MW-N: Challenge causes positive changes; friction in life changes overcome through gathered wisdom

MW-W: Increased knowledge emphasized, resulting in opportunities/positive changes/new life

MW-E: Wisdom harvested; prosperity from knowledge; opportunity for gains from education/learning

MW-S: Contentment from gathered knowledge and positive changes; harmony in life changes

UW-N: Ending of harmony; transformation through gathered knowledge and wisdom emphasized; rapid changes for the better

UW-W: Knowledge increases capacity for love/pleasure; wisdom in love; opportunity in love; positive changes in love/pleasure

UW-E: Growth of opportunity; increase in positive changes; youthful approach to life

UW-S: Energy to implement life changes; vitality of knowledge and wisdom; energetic changes

14. ⊥⊥ Truth/Endurance/Strength—Path to Underworld

Duir in the following placements:

OW-N: Endurance of wisdom; longevity

OW-W: Inspiration of truth; willpower brings peace

OW-E: Abundance through strength/willpower

OW-S: Happiness found in truth/inner strength

MW-N: Able to endure challenges; overcome obstacles

MW-W: Learning truth; overcome obstacles to learning; strength in knowledge

MW-E: Endurance/willpower brings results; prosperity in truth; solid achievements

MW-S: Contentment from overcoming obstacles; harmony in truth; creating own contentment through willpower

UW-N: Positive force applied to create transformation; Ending of obstacles; truth revealed

UW-W: Use of determination to secure love; truth in love; love conquers all

UW-E: Ability to overcome obstacles leads to growth; growth through willpower; youthful strength

UW-S: Vitality of truth; energy to overcome obstacles; energy enhances strength; vitality of willpower

15. ⚹ Developing Skills/Learning—Path to Underworld

Gort in the following placements:

OW-N: Gains in due time; increasing wisdom

OW-W: Peace comes through tenacity; inspired to learning; new skills discovered

OW-E: Abundance by persistence; developing skills lead to favorable results; learning brings gains

OW-S: Joy of learning; happiness is attained by tenacity

MW-N: Challenge in persistence; friction leads to new skills developed; difficult studies

MW-W: Learning emphasized; learning involves new skills; gains in knowledge through hard work/tenacity

MW-E: Prosperity from new skills; gains from persistence

MW-S: Contentment found in new skills/learning; harmony comes with effort and persistence

UW-N: Hard work pays off; persistence transforms into tangible gains; transformation through learning

UW-W: Pleasure in a new skill/learning; persistence in love succeeds

UW-E: Growth from learning; growth of skills; gains in youth through persistence

UW-S: Energy to gain goals through tenacity; vitality of learning; energy to develop skills

16. ᚈ Insight/Foreknowledge/Enlivening—Path to Underworld

Luis in the following placements:

OW-N: Insight in age; ability in foreknowledge enhanced

OW-W: Healing; inspiration enhances creativity

OW-E: Abundance of insight; power of healing; great activity

OW-S: Happiness in creativity; able to find own bliss; relief; using insight to bring happiness; joyfully active

MW-N: Challenge leads to increase in activity; argument clears the air; friction in creativity; insight leads to friction

MW-W: Learning healing; knowledge of healing; insightfulness; creative learning

MW-E: Prosperity from insight/healing; foreknowledge used wisely; successful creativity; fruitful activity

MW-S: Contentment in creativity; insight brings contentment; harmonious activity

UW-N: Transformation from insight; endings/new beginnings brought about through healing; new activities

UW-W: Healing love; insightfulness in love; creativity brings pleasure

UW-E: Youthful activities; growth of insight; creativity enhanced

UW-S: Energy for activities; vitality of insight; healing energy

17. ᚈ Rulership/Vigor/Discernment

Ailm in the following placements:

OW-N: Discretion in wisdom; vigor in age; secret wisdom

OW-W: Secret inspiration; discretion in peace

OW-E: Discrete use of bounty; vigorous abundance

OW-S: Discretion ensures happiness; happiness in rulership; vigor in bliss

MW-N: Challenge met with discrete rulership; vigorous response; secrecy breeds friction

MW-W: Learning discretion; secret knowledge; aptitude for learning; leader in education

MW-E: Prosperous rulership; gains from discretion/secrecy; vitality in prosperity

MW-S: Harmony from discretion; contentment in rulership

UW-N: Secrecy leads to transformation; new openness; transformation of rulership

UW-W: Secret love; discretion in pleasure; vigorous love; dominance in love

UW-E: Growth of rulership; growth of discretion/secrecy; youthful vigor

UW-S: Vigor emphasized; energy for rulership

18. ⊥ Pleasure/Misfortune/Cleansing

Huath in the following placements:

OW-N: Pleasure in wisdom; comfortable old age; positive changes in age

OW-W: Inspirational cleansing; stimulating peace; positivity

OW-E: Enjoyment of abundance

OW-S: Cleansing brings happiness

MW-N: Challenge/friction may lead to misfortune or positive changes

MW-W: Knowledge leads to positive changes; pleasure in learning

MW-E: Harvest what is sown as either pleasure or misfortune; prosperity from positive changes/cleansing

MW-S: Harmony emphasized; contentment from cleansing

UW-N: Endings bring a positive change; transformation through cleansing

UW-W: Pleasure emphasized; enjoyment of love; care needed to avoid misfortune in love

UW-E: Growth of pleasure; youthful pleasures; growth brings cleansing

UW-S: Energy for positive changes; vitality for pleasure

19. ⫫ Introspection/Other Sight

Muin in the following placements:

OW-N: Introspection in age; introspective wisdom

OW-W: Inspiration from introspection; peace through reflection

OW-E: Bounty from other sight; introspection leads to abundance
OW-S: Happiness from looking inward
MW-N: Challenge in self-analysis; friction leads to introspection
MW-W: Learning through introspection/reflection; knowledge comes from within/from other sight
MW-E: Rewards reaped from reflection/introspection
MW-S: Contentment found by introspection; harmony based upon reflection
UW-N: Transformed by introspection/other sight
UW-W: Introspective approach to love
UW-E: Growth from looking inward
UW-S: Energy turned to introspection; reflective youth

20. T Beginnings/Energy

Beithe in the following placements:

OW-N: Beginnings of wisdom; energetic age
OW-W: Beginnings of inspiration; unseen forces lead to inspiration and peace
OW-E: Abundant energy; auspicious beginnings
OW-S: Happiness from new beginning; energy for bliss
MW-N: Challenge pushes for new beginning; energy from friction
MW-W: Beginning of learning/knowledge; energy for learning; subtle growth of knowledge
MW-E: Beginning of period of prosperity; energy to bring matters to fruition
MW-S: Contentment from new beginnings; harmony with the unseen forces of growth
UW-N: Ending leads to a new beginning; transformative energy; transformed by growth
UW-W: Beginning of love/pleasure; unseen forces of growth at work in love; energy for love/pleasure
UW-E: Growth emphasized; youthful energy; growth leads to new beginning
UW-S: Energy emphasized; vitality in new beginning; vitality of quiet growth

21. —— Cosmic Influence/Destiny/Fate

Blank in all worlds and realms shows the cosmic influence in that world and realm; destiny or fate expressed in that world and realm Blank in the following placements:

OW-N: Age; wisdom
OW-W: Gentleness; inspiration
OW-E: Abundance
OW-S: Happiness
MW-N: Conflict; resistance; challenge
MW-W: Learning; knowledge
MW-E: Prosperity; harvest
MW-S: Harmony; contentment
MW-M: Central focus
UW-N: Endings; transformation
UW-W: Love
UW-E: Growth
UW-S: Vitality; energy

The midhes are the centers of the three worlds of the Celtic cosmology, and act as the passage point for travel between the light of Otherworld and dark of Underworld.

— Spell —
Passing the Midhes

This spell combines ritual, meditation, spellwork, and a charm to draw the power of both the light and dark aspects together to aid in spiritual development. Read it through and see what you may want to alter or add. The midhes are the centers of the three worlds of the Celtic cosmology, and act as the passage point for travel between the light of Otherworld and dark of Underworld.

Ritual Bath

Begin with a ritual bath as previously described, but this time, scented with lavender and vervain. Lavender opens the psychic centers and attracts the attention of the Other People. Vervain opens the psychic centers, attracts good luck, and enhances creativity. Both herbs are used for happiness and peace, protection, and offerings to the Ancient Ones. Both are herbs of purification that, when included in your bath and in scented candles around your bath, help prepare you for spellwork. After your bath you may want to dress in something loose and comfortable.

What You Will Need

Arrange your ritual area to include three pillar candles in a horizontal line across the altar (your altar might be table-sized or a could be a large area on the ground or floor): one white, one red, and one black. These colors are the traditional colors of the Triple Goddess, symbolizing Maiden, Mother, and Crone. These colors also represent the three worlds of the cosmos of Otherworld-Middleworld-Underworld.

Cover the top of your altar area with a green cloth to represent the herbal earth of Green Witchcraft. I like to use the sheer scarf with patterns of dark green leaves and accents of gold and black described earlier in my shopping adventure with the Elementals.

The altar should have the three candles, a candle snuffer, a small cauldron, a pentacle (I prefer one on wood or tile for heat resistance), an incense burner that you can carry around the circle (with a handle or chains, for example), acacia herb (to drop onto a charcoal incense disk) or lavender incense in stick or cone variety, spring water, an anointing oil, matches, something to eat and drink (such as a cornbread muffin and chalice of white wine or light-colored fruit drink), black mirror, burdock root, marigold (calendula), mullein (graveyard dust), your ogham fews (for focus and empowerment), a 3-inch x 5-inch piece of paper (or parchment), pen and ink (I like to write spells in dragon's blood ink, which can be found in magical supply stores and mail order), three 12-inch lengths of thread in red, purple, and green, and a purple (lavender) candle (a small votive is best) in a holder.

You will also need your ritual knife and a wand. The best wood for a wand in this spell is one of hazel. The magical association of hazel is wisdom and the witch, and this helps to keep the work focused on the journey of the witch rather than on the worlds or the aspects of the deities. The symbolic bird of the hazel is the crane, and in the Celtic tradition, the "crane-dance" was the method used to travel to the worlds, and the ogham fews were kept in a bag of crane-skin. Have your own collection of ogham fews on the altar.

On the purple candle, inscribe the symbols for the Lady and the Lord—these may be the horned circle for the Lord and the circle flanked by crescent moons for the Lady, or you may use runic or other symbols. Inscribe the candle with the symbols for travel (a wide M) and between the worlds (a squarish hourglass figure laying on its side).

On your green cloth, place the black mirror at the center of the altar with your ogham fews behind the mirror and the three pillar candles set across the front (black-red-white), along with the burdock, marigold, and mullein herbs, and the pentacle.

Set the purple votive at the upper right portion of the altar (the God area), along with the incense (acacia or lavender), and holder. The water goes at the upper left portion of the altar (the Goddess area), along with the small cauldron and the cup of juice or wine. If you have deity figurines, these enhance the appearance and feel of the altar and can be placed in the appropriate areas with the objects in front of them.

Beginning the Spell

Light the incense and the purple (or lavender) altar candle. If using a charcoal diskette, light it and place some of the acacia on it to smolder.

Cast your circle beginning at the North, as is usual in Green Witchcraft. You should be facing North as you work your spell. Make yourself comfortable. If this means your altar is a table you sit at, that is fine. First you will sweep the area to be made your sacred space. Then you create the circle, call upon the Elementals, invoke the Divine, and proceed into the spellwork. When finished, you have a bit of refreshment, give and receive the blessings of the Divine, farewell the Elementals, open the circle, and put away your tools.

Casting the Circle

Sweep the circle area with a besom (your witch's broom made of straw, grass, or other material, but not Scotch broom as the odor is offensive to the Other People) clockwise, starting at the North and moving to the East, South, West, and returning to the North, saying as you go:

> *As I sweep, may the Besom chase away all negativity from within this circle, that it be cleansed and ready for my work.*

The circle may be large or small; delineated with a cord, drawn in the dirt, or simply visualized. The Quarters of North, East, South, and West may be defined by candles in heat-proof dishes—green, yellow, red, and blue respectively for Earth, Air, Fire, and Water.

Clap your hands three times and say:

> *The circle is about to be cast and I freely stand within to greet my Lady and my Lord.*

Walk around your sacred space with your wand (elder, oak, hazel, or ash are best) pointing at the ground to delineate the circle, and as you create the circle, say:

The circle is drawn as a **Circle of Power** *around me, above me, and below me in a sphere that passes through all boundaries in all planes.*

Return to your altar and place the point of the athame (your ritual knife) in the burdock root (it represents both Middleworld and *cleansing*, and here works as a *grounding* herb), and say:

Burdock root is the Lord's herb of purification, protection, and warding of the negative. I bless this herb to be used in this sacred circle in the names of the Goddess and the God (_____ and _____).

Pick up a bit of burdock root (you will need some for the spell) with the tip of the athame and drop three portions of root into the bowl of spring water. Stir three times with the athame and say:

Let this blessed root purify this water that it may be blessed to use in this sacred circle. In the names of the Goddess and the God, (_____ and _____), I consecrate and cleanse this water.

Take the water bowl in hand and sprinkle water from it as you move deosil around the circle (N-E-S-W), and say:

This circle is cleansed by the water and earth.

Return the water bowl to the altar and take up the incense. Walk around the ring and waft the incense smoke with your hand, a dark feather, or an herbal sprig (such as heather), and say:

This circle, purified by fragrance and smoke, is sealed in the Names of the Goddess and the God, (_____ and _____), Only love shall enter and leave.

Take anointing oil and on your forehead make a Solar Cross (equal-armed), then over it make the Lunar Spiral and say:

I, (Craft Name or Working Name), am consecrated in the names of the Goddess and the God, (_____ and _____), in this their circle.

Calling the Elementals

Set the incense on the altar, and take up the purple candle. Light the candles set at the Quarters as you progress around the circle, first greeting the Elemental, then lighting the candle. Begin at the North of the circle and say:

> *I welcome thee, Elemental Earth, to my circle. As I am of flesh and bone, we are kith and kin, and I call upon you to watch over me, aid, and guide me in my travels.*

Light the North candle. Move to the East and say:

> *I welcome thee, Elemental Air, to my circle. As I am of thought and breath, we are kith and kin, and I call upon you to watch over me, aid, and guide me in my travels.*

Light the East candle. Move to the South and say:

> *I welcome thee, Elemental Fire, to my circle. As I am of heat and energy, we are kith and kin, and I call upon you to watch over me, aid, and guide me in my travels.*

Light the South candle. Move to the West and say:

> *I welcome thee, Elemental Water, to my circle. As I am of water and blood, we are kith and kin, and I call upon you to watch over me, aid, and guide me in my travels.*

Light the West candle and return to the altar, setting down the purple candle. Use the wand to draw in the air above the altar, the symbol of Infinity (a figure 8 laying on its side)—the sign of working between the worlds.

Set your wand on the altar, raise up both hands, and say:

> *Hail to the Elementals at the Four Quarters! Welcome Lady and Lord to this rite! I stand between the worlds with Love and Power all around!*

Set down the athame and pick up the goblet. Pour a little into the cauldron as a libation, and take a sip.

Passing the Midhes Spell

The focus of this spell is ease in passage between the worlds at their intersection points. Of the four paths to Otherworld and four paths to Underworld, coll (⊥⊥) and duir (⊥⊥) are the ones used in this spell. You may choose another path that has relevance to you, but coll, the hazel, connects the power of wisdom with the wand and the practitioner, and duir, the oak, connects the power of courage with the seeking of truth.

Take the red candle and light it from the purple one, then set it on top of the pentacle in front of the black mirror, and say:

> *Here I stand in the center of my world, passionate of life and physical of form.*

Drop some of the burdock into the red candle flame and affirm your place on this plane by saying:

> *The Middleworld of challenge, knowledge, prosperity, and contentment bring me joy.*

Now, write along the upper-right top edge of the paper the path few for coll for your travel to Otherworld. Think about the properties of this tree as the witches' tree, the tree of wicce, or wisdom, creativity, and perception. Then say:

> *I call upon the spirit of the hazel to be my guide and open the path to me to Otherworld.*

Crease the paper and pass it through the incense smoke and sprinkle it lightly with the blessed water; pass it quickly through the red candle flame, saying:

> *By Earth and by Air; by Water and by Fire, I call upon the power of coll to guide me. I have the passage of hazel in my hand!*

Snap shut the section of paper with the few on it and fold the paper over tightly. Hold onto this with one hand and with the other, light the white candle from the red one and say the following:

With coll do I pass the midhe from Middleworld to Otherworld.

Move the red candle to the right side and place the white candle in front of the black mirror. Gaze into the mirror past the flame and envision the path to Otherworld blocked by hazel branches. Lightly tap the mirror with the folded paper and say:

Open the midhe, for I have coll in my hand.

See the branches part. See the path that lies before you, and that your paper is transformed into a wand of hazel. Drop some of the marigold into the white candle flame and say:

I give the gift of calendula to receive the gift of sight in Otherworld. Let this herb open the way as an offering to the People of this fair world.

You move along the path, through a woodland, and enter into a broad plain in which you can see that there are four realms spreading outward from the point where you stand at their meeting. Say:

Here I stand in the center of Otherworld, filled with the wonder of eternity, and spiritual in form.

Point the hazel wand (paper with the few) in each quarter, one at a time, saying as you do so:

I move with coll in the North (and see what is shown to you of age and wisdom).

Then:

I move with coll in the West (and see what is shown to you of light and gentleness).

Then:

I move with coll in the East (and see what is shown to you of abundance).

Then:

I move with coll in the South (and see what is shown to you of happiness).

Return now to the midhe and say:

I take the passage of coll back to Middleworld.

Carefully set the white candle back at the right side and place the red candle before the mirror. See yourself moving back along the path through the woods and back into your own place at the altar.

With the paper still folded over the few of coll, write now the few symbol of duir, the oak, in the upper left space for your travel to Underworld. Think about the properties of this tree as power, endurance, truth, and strength. Then say:

I call upon the spirit of the oak to be my guide and open the path to me to Underworld.

Crease the paper and pass it through the symbols of the Elementals, (incense smoke, light sprinkle of blessed water mixed with burdock, and the votive candle flame), saying:

By Earth and by Air, by Water and by Fire, I call upon the power of duir to guide me. I have the passage of oak in my hand!

Snap shut the section of paper with this few on it and fold the paper tightly over once more. Hold onto this with one hand, and with the other light the black candle from the red one, and say:

With duir do I pass the midhe from Middleworld to Underworld.

Move the red candle to the right side and place the black candle in front of the black mirror. Gaze into the mirror past the flame and envision the path to Underworld blocked by low-spreading branches of river oaks. Lightly tap the mirror with the folded paper and say:

Open the midhe, for I have duir in my hand.

See the branches part. See the dark river that lies before you, and see that your paper is transformed into a wand of oak. Drop some of the mullein into the black candle flame and say:

I give the gift of mullein to receive the gift of sight in Underworld. Let this herb open the way as an offering to the People of this shadow world.

You step into a small flatboat and move across the placid river to land on the opposite shadowy shore. You step out of the boat and enter into a plain in which you can see that there are four realms spreading outward from the point where you stand at their meeting. Say:

Here I stand in the center of Underworld, serene with love and transformation, fleeting of form.

Point the oak wand (paper with the few) in each quarter, one at a time, saying as you do so:

I move with duir in the North (and see what is shown to you of death and transformation).

Then:

I move with duir in the West (and see what is shown to you of the cleansing and positive changes).

Then:

I move with duir in the East (and see what is shown to you of introspection, growth, and fruition).

Then:

I move with duir in the South (and see what is shown to you of energy, new beginnings, and hidden powers).

Return now to the midhe and say:

I take the passage of duir back to Middleworld.

Carefully set the black candle back at the left side and return the red candle before the mirror. See yourself moving back to the river, boarding the boat, and crossing the dark river. You are now back into your own place at the altar.

Now look into the mirror past the flame of the red candle. Bend the folded paper so both ends point forward, and see yourself holding two wands in your hand, one of hazel and one of oak. Say:

> *The midhes stand open, for I have coll and duir,*
> *Wisdom and Strength, in my hand.*

Drop some of the burdock into the red candle flame and say:

> *I give the gift of burdock to receive the gift of sight in*
> *Middleworld. Let this herb open the way as an offering*
> *to the powers of this land.*

See the realms of Middleworld spreading from the point where you stand at the center where they touch.

> *Here I stand once more, in the center of my world,*
> *Passionate of life and physical of form.*

Point the double wand to each quarter, one at a time, saying as you do so:

> *I move with Wisdom and Strength in the North, to*
> *learn from challenges and overcome obstacles* (and
> see what is shown to you of gateways to success and
> self-expression).

Then:

> *I move with Wisdom and Strength in the West, to gain*
> *in knowledge and learning* (and see what is shown to
> you of tests to come, balance, and decisions to be made).

Then:

> *I move with Wisdom and Strength in the East, to*
> *achieve prosperity and harvest* (and see what is shown
> to you of inner transformations and development for
> harmony).

127

Then:

I move with Wisdom and Strength in the South, to know contentment with the strength to enjoy life (and see what is shown to you of inner strength, awareness, and confidence).

Midhe Charm

Now hold the doubled paper folded tightly together and say:

Here have I the paths opened from Middleworld to Otherworld and Underworld that I move between the worlds with ease of passage.

Wrap the red thread around the paper and say:

Let the power of red enhance the strength of the oak.

Wrap the purple thread around the paper and say:

Let the power of purple enhance the wisdom of the hazel.

Wrap the green thread around the paper and say:

Let the power of green enhance this tool with the herbal blessing of Nature.

Place the wrapped paper into a small black pouch and close (drawstring and tied or gathered and wrapped with black thread) and pass through the symbols of the Elementals (incense smoke, flame of the purple candle, sprinkled with the water mixed with burdock), then say:

My wand of coll and duir I keep close to me,
Passed through the Elementals, warded in black from negativity and knotted thrice: (tie each knot as you continue) *once for Otherworld, once for Underworld, and once for Middleworld. The passing of the Midhes lies in my hands.*

128

Put your ogham fews on top of the pentacle and lay the pouch on top of the fews, then snuff the white, black, and red candles. Leave the pouch on the altar one hour, then put the charm in your ogham bag.

Cakes and Wine

I appreciate my needs and that which sustains me!
May I ever remember the blessings of my Lady and
my Lord.

Take up the goblet in left hand and athame in right. Slowly lower the point of the knife into the wine (or fruit juice) and say:

As male joins female for the happiness of both, let
the fruit of Divine Union promote life. Let the Earth
be fruitful and let her wealth be spread throughout
all lands.

Lay down the athame, pour a little of the drink into the cauldron, and then drink from the cup. Replace the goblet on the altar and pick up the athame. Touch the point of the knife to the cornbread muffin or cake in the offering dish and say:

This food is the blessing of the Lady and the Lord given
freely to me. As freely as I have received, may I also
give food for the body, mind, and spirit to those who
seek such of me.

Take a small portion of the muffin or cake and drop it into the cauldron, then eat the rest and finish the drink, saying:

As I enjoy these gifts of the Goddess and the God,
(_____ and _____), may I remember that without them
I would have nothing. So Mote It Be!

Blessings and Farewells

When all is finished, hold the athame in power hand level over altar and say:

129

*Lord and Lady, I am blessed by your sharing this time
with me; watching and guarding me, and guiding me
here and in all things. I came in love and I depart
in love.*

Raise up the athame in a salute:

*Love is the law and love is the bond. Merry did I meet,
merry do I part, and merry will I meet again. Merry
meet, merry part, and merry meet again! The circle is
now cleared. So Mote It Be!*

Kiss the flat of the blade and set the athame on the altar. Take up
the snuffer and go to the North Quarter, raise up your arms:

*Depart in peace, Elemental Earth.
My blessings take with you!*

Lower your arms and snuff the candle; envision the Elemental
Power departing.

Go to the East, raise up your arms:

*Depart in peace, Elemental Air.
My blessings take with you!*

Lower your arms and snuff the candle; envision the Elemental
Power departing.

Go to the South, raise up your arms:

*Depart in peace, Elemental Fire.
My blessings take with you!*

Lower your arms and snuff the candle; envision the Elemental
Power departing.

Go to the West, raise up your arms:

*Depart in peace, Elemental Water.
My blessings take with you!*

Lower your arms and snuff the candle; envision the Elemental
Power departing.

Return to altar and set down the snuffer. Raise up your arms:

> *Beings and powers of the visible and invisible, depart in peace! You aid in my work, whisper in my mind, and bless me from Otherworld, and there is harmony between us. My blessings take with you. The circle is cleared.*

Touch the palms of your hands to the ground to drain off any excess energy from your spellwork. Now you are ready to open the circle.

Opening the Circle

Take up the wand and go to the North, point the wand down and move widdershins (counterclockwise) around circle (N-W-S-E), envisioning the blue light drawing back into the athame:

> *The circle is open yet the circle remains as its magical power is drawn back into me.*

Return to the altar, raise up the wand with your arms outstretched, and say:

> *The ceremony is ended. Blessings have been given and Blessings have been received, may the peace of the Goddess and the God remain in my heart. So Mote It Be!*

Set down the wand, put away all magical tools, and clear the altar. The cauldron contents is poured onto the Earth. You may use the water of this ritual as holy water to sprinkle around your home as a blessing, or store it for use in other spells and blessings.

7

What Are Dark Power Herbal Magics?

Working with the Dark Powers

Herbs and oils are typically used in rituals, spells, charms, and other magics of witchcraft, but some are more suited than others for connecting with the dark powers. A listing of herbs with their magical associations and properties was given in *Green Witchcraft*, and these can be adapted to any type of magical activity. But what about herbs that can be specifically related to dark power magics? In this chapter is a sample list of dark power herbs. Be aware that a few of these are poisonous and should not be handled, inhaled, or ingested. They are included here as a historical reference only.

While some herbs may be used in teas, this listing is intended for such magical workings as meditations, rituals, spells, and charms. Teas have been suggested for some of the meditations already. I like to add burdock root and elder flowers to teas for flavor and for their magical properties, and I have given several of my favorite herbal tea recipes in the earlier book. I was taught that black teas add power, so my recipes are usually based on hearty black teas such as Irish Breakfast, English Breakfast and Teatime, China Rose, and Earl Grey with milk and a touch of sugar added.

Magical oils are easily made by soaking herbs in a light oil of saffron or sunflower, bottled and stored away from light. These oils bring the power of the herbs into magical practice and personal connection, and may be used to anoint a tool when consecrating it for magical use. Oils are used in ritual for self-consecration, in the dedication of objects, in spells (called dressing when used on the items for spells, such as on inscribed candles), charms, meditations, or other purposes. Some of the familiar essential oils that are easy to find in stores (particularly stores specializing in health foods or occult supplies) are: acacia, balsam, fir, gorse, hyssop, jasmine, lavender, nettle, patchouli, rosemary, St. John's wort, thistle, thyme, valerian, vetiver, and yarrow.

Herbs may also be soaked in spring water, and then the water is blessed and used for ritual cleansing of the altar, magic area, rooms, and house. House blessings usually are done at Imbolc, but the Sabbats of the seasonal changes—Yule (December 21), Ostara (March 21), Litha (June 21), and Mabon (September21)— may also be times for asperging to keep the house in balance with the *turning of the wheel.* The herbal water may be sprinkled with the use of a sprig of heather or other herb chosen for its inherent magical properties.

Dark power herbs are those with an additional attunement to death, passage, transitions, rebirth, Underworld or Shadowland, Otherworld, and to aspects and divinities identified with the Crone and the Hunter. They enhance the powers of the dark Sabbats and dark Esbats, and are excellent for magics of the solar and lunar eclipses.

What Are Dark Power Herbal Magics?

Some of these herbs have great power to *return-to-sender* harmful intent and negativity that was specifically sent. Others, indicated as *deflection*, will defuse general malevolence or ill will from others, while *retribution* will return energy to its generator with the added energy of the herb sealing it there. Blackthorn and elder can be used in *curses*, but these should not be stress-related dark magics, because *what is sent comes back*. In other words, the intent of the witch is what matters. The best use of such herbs could be to contain malevolence to the sphere occupied by the generator, for example.

Exorcism herbs may be used to aid spirits in their passage, but are more generally used to disperse negative energies. Samhain rituals sometimes contain a call to troubled or confused spirits so that they may be aided during the ritual to move on to Shadowland. These spells are very powerful and should only be undertaken when you have had sufficient experience, since often there is a very large upswelling of flame and psychic energy. Spirit exorcism is not for the faint of heart or the timid, not because of any belligerence of witch or spirits, but because of the strong psychic energies.

The usual purpose of exorcism, however, is to clear out negative energies and allow positive energies to enter a space. This is helpful when moving into a new home, especially if there was anger or violence in the area at one time. It is also good for censing a house after unpleasant guests have left. Exorcism allows you to clear out doubts and frustrations so that you can have a fresh start in your work and relationships. The purposes for exorcism in the Green Craft are not the same as portrayed in most popular literature and movies.

Purgings and *releasing* spells are lesser exorcisms that invoke the energies of the herbs to cleanse and turn away negativity. They can also absorb negativity and then be buried in order for the energy to be grounded and dissipated. Some of the things you can do with this kind of energy are to seek aid in turning away from bad habits, releasing obstacles to your development, and clearing out impediments to success. New or Dark Moon Esbat rituals can include this kind of spell work.

Herbal Correspondences

Absinthe: Crone, Dark Moon, Lunar Eclipse, Underworld

Acacia: inspiration, protection, Lughnassadh passage, psychic power,

Agrimony: exorcism, sleep, calming, protection, return-to-sender

Amaranth (cockscomb): death passage, Samhain, immortality, spirit communication

Anise: Crone, protection, purification, psychic power, divination, seeking answers, spirit contact, deflection of negativity

Apple: Underworld, rebirth, immortality, food for the dead, Samhain

Artemesia: Dark Lady, Dark Moon, Lunar Eclipse

Asafetida: bad-smelling resin used for exorcism and protection

Ash (bark/leaves): death, passage, Beltane, protection, health, prophecy, insight, dreams

Avens: exorcism, purification

Balsam: Underworld passage, psychic energy, spirit communication

Bay: Yule, Imbolc, psychic power, strength, purification, healing

Bayberry: [poisonous] scented candles okay for Yule, transition

Belladonna (Deadly Nightshade): [all parts are poisonous, use Dittany of Crete or Mugwort instead] Samhain, astral travel, psychic power, visions

Blackberry: Dark Lord, Lughnassadh, Hunter, protection

Black Currant (cassis): Lord of Shadows, Hunter, Wild Hunt

Blackthorn: defense, deflect negativity, retribution, protection, Otherworld contact

Boneset: deflection, exorcism, protection

Briar: defense, protection, enhance witch's power, divination, dreams

Burdock: wards negativity, purification, protection

Clove: banishing/releasing, exorcism, protection, companion offering

Cypress: banishing/releasing, binding, death, immortality, eternity, Hades, Underworld, Hecate, Shadowland

Damiana: visions, healing

Dandelion (root): psychic power, spirit contact, Otherworld

Dianthus (carnation): protection, power, health, blood, regeneration

Dittany of Crete: astral travel, spirit communication

Dragon's Blood (palm resin): binding, changes, courage, energy, strength, power, exorcism, protection

136

Elder: Crone, banishing/releasing, defense, deflection, retribution, Litha, blessings, wards negativity, Otherworld, protection, visions, spirit contact, occult learning, healing, exorcism

Elecampane (elfdock): psychic power, protection, divination, Otherworld contact

Elm (elvin): protection, attraction, energy

Fennel: protection, purification, healing, ward negativity,
Fern: banishing/releasing, exorcism, protection, Samhain, Otherworld
Fir: Yule, Underworld
Foxglove: [poisonous, use Tamarisk instead] defense, protection, return to sender, deflection
Frankincense: anointing, strength, power, energy, exorcism, Yule, Beltane, Lughnassadh, protection, consecration, visions

Garlic: protection, ward negativity, Dark Lady (Hecate), exorcism, healing
Ginger (root): psychic power, protection, exorcism, deflection, return-to-sender, drawing, spirit contact
Gorse (furze): protection, preparation for conflict

Hawthorn: protection, enhance witch's power, Otherworld, Beltane, wards negativity, attract Fairies
Hazel: invoke Otherworld aid, attract Fair Folk, enhance witch's power
Hellebore: [poisonous, use Black Currant instead] Crone, Lord of Shadows, Underworld, visions, psychic power, exorcism, astral travel
Hemlock: [poison, use Lilac instead] power, purification, protection, astral travel
Henbane: [poisonous, use Mace instead] Underworld, spirit contact
Holly: [poisonous, use Frankincense instead] energy, strength, power, insight, protection, deflection
Hyssop: protection, purification, cleansing, removes negativity and malevolence

Jasmine: anointing, balance, Ostara, divination, dreams, insight, astral projection
Jimsonweed (datura): [poison, use Agrimony instead] deflection, return-to-sender, ward negativity, protection

Juniper Berry: visions, purification, spirit contact, exorcism, protection

Lady's Slipper: wards negative energy, return-to-sender, protection, deflection

Lavender (elf leaf): anointing, exorcism, purification, Litha, honoring Ancient Ones, protection, cleansing, Otherworld, Sidhe contact, opening psychic centers, spirit contact

Lilac: Underworld, Beltane, exorcism, protection, cleansing

Linden: immortality, protection, Underworld

Mace: psychic power, enhance spirit contact, Underworld

Mandrake: [poisonous, use Ginger Root or Fennel Root instead] calling upon spirits, communication with the dead, spirit offering, exorcism, protective watcher

Marigold (calendula): divination, Otherworld, Fairy offering, Beltane, Mabon, protection, dreams, psychic power

Mastic: spirit contact, enhance psychic power, strength

May-apple: [poisonous, use Ginger Root or Fennel Root instead] spirit contact, death, spirit offering, substitute for mandrake

Mugwort (artemesia): Dark Lady, Dark Moon, Lunar Eclipse, psychic power, dreams, banishing/releasing, divination, cleansing magic mirrors and crystal balls, Litha, astral projection, strength, protection, healing

Mullein: Crone energy, courage, exorcism, "graveyard dust," divination, protection, return-to-sender, deflection

Myrrh: Imbolc, Mabon, exorcism, protection, purification, power

Nettle: protection, exorcism, return to sender, deflection, courage

Oak (galls/leaves/wood): strength, power purification, charms, Mabon, Samhain, Yule

Orris Root: power, protection, divination, deflection

Paprika: protection, wards malevolent energy, deflection

Patchouli: Samhain, Underworld, passage

Pennyroyal: [poisonous, use Blackthorn instead] deflection, power, protection, ward negative energy

Peppercorn: protection, power, deflection, exorcism

Pomegranate: Underworld, passage, hidden wealth, attainment, protection, deflection, secret knowledge

Purple Heather: peace, cleansing, spiritual attainment, Samhain, Imbolc, Lughnassadh

Rosemary (elf leaf): courage, exorcism, protection, purification, dreams, health, strength, cleansing, Otherworld, Sidhe contact

Rowan Wood (Mountain Ash): [berries are poisonous] binding, divination, secret knowledge, divination, calling upon spirits, calling upon the Sidhe for aid, psychic power, protection,

Rue: [poisonous, use Tamarisk instead] exorcism, health, enhance magics, return-to-sender, deflection, retribution, ward malevolence and negative energies

Sage: Yule, Mabon, immortality, wisdom, protection, spirit and Otherworld offering, exorcism, purification

Sandalwood: meditation, intuitive power, protection, spirit contact, exorcism

Skullcap: protection, healing, passage to Underworld

St. John's wort: [poisonous, use Elder instead] banishing/releasing, Otherworld, Midsummer (Litha), power, protection

Tamarisk (flowering cypress): exorcism, divination, deflection, return-to-sender

Tansy: [poisonous, use Elder or Hazel instead instead] Dark Goddess, immortality, flowers for Otherworld offering

Thistle: protection, warding/changing bad luck, Mabon, exorcism, deflection of negative energies, return-to-sender, spirit contact

Thyme: ward negativity, Litha, protection, psychic power, healing, purification, Otherworld

Tumeric: protection, cleansing, purification

Turnip: Samhain lanterns, ward negative energies, protection, passage, rebirth

Unicorn Root (ague root): protection, return-to-sender, exorcism

Valerian: power, purging, releasing, protection, purification

Vervain (verbena): purification, cleansing, protection, psychic power, strength, anointing, exorcism, offerings, open psychic centers, creativity, Underworld riches, guidance, dreams, divination, Otherworld contact, luck

Vetiver: deflection, ward malevolence, retribution

Willow: Hecate, death, Underworld, passage, protection, spirit contact, deflection

Woodruff: changes, Herne, clear barriers, overcome obstacles, Beltane, protection

Wormwood: [poisonous, use Mugwort or Cypress instead] binding, divination, exorcism, Samhain, divination, spirit evocation, protection, Dark Moon, Lunar Eclipse, dreams, psychic power

Yarrow (arrowroot): exorcism, releasing, divination, psychic power, protection, dreams, guidance, courage

Yew: [poisonous, use Sandalwood or Skullcap instead] spirit contact, transitions, death/rebirth, Underworld, Yule

Using Dark Power Herbs

Many of the nonpoisonous herbs can be added to candle flames during spellwork, but wormwood requires good ventilation. Dark power herbs are used to honor the Divine, the Sidhe, and the Elementals at rituals dedicated to them or seeking their aid. These herbs are also used in the cleansing and dedication of dark power tools in rituals such as shown earlier. Spells and candle magics, charms, and washes are other uses. Some spells have already been shown with accompanying rituals and meditations, but charms can also be made, such as the one for the Elemental Bottle.

Poisonous herbs have traditionally been used to strengthen charms and spells, but even handling some of these herbs can be dangerous; the toxins may be absorbed through the skin. Nonpoiosonous herbal substitutes are recommended.

Incenses are derived from a number of herbs, flowers, roots, and nuts as listed above, so that you can select the herbs you want for a purpose, and match the incense and any oil needed accordingly. The practice of the Craft is rather like choosing from a menu of options. There are herbs that can be burned in a candle, stuffed into a dream pillow, added to an object, rubbed onto a tool or spell item, or sewn up into a charm. There are incenses to enhance the atmosphere for the intended purpose of the Craft work, and there are herbal oils to dress candles, tools, and objects in magical practice.

Herbs for the Elementals

These are herbs that specifically invoke and focus on the powers of the Elementals. They can be offerings given to honor the essences of life and of ourselves, and can be used to enhance awareness of our kinship. Both light and dark power herbs are listed here.

Earth: material matters; physical form; wealth; career

Balm of Gilead	Fern	Mandrake
Bistort	High John the Conqueror	Patchouli
Cedar	Honeysuckle	Pine
Cinquefoil	Horehound	Sage
Clove	Jasmine	Slippery Elm

Air: intellect; mind; creativity; breath; visions; psychic power

Acacia	Eucalyptus	Mastic	Spearmint
Anise	Eyebright	Mistletoe	Thyme
Benzoin	Hazel	Mugwort	Wormwood
Broom	Lavender	Nutmeg	
Comfrey	Lemon Verbena	Peppermint	
Elder	Marjoram	Sandalwood	

Fire: will; passion; divine within; energy; protection; healing

Alder	Cinnamon	Marigold	Saffron
Angelica	Coriander	Peony	St. John's wort
Basil	Cumin	Pepper	Thistle
Bay Laurel	Garlic	Primrose	Vervain
Betony	Holly	Rosemary	
Carnation	Hyssop	Rowan	
Celadine	Juniper	Rue	

Water: emotions; subconscious; dreams; purification; blood; fluids

Apple	Catnip	Ivy	Poppy
Ash	Elecampane	Lovage	Rose
Burdock	Geranium	Meadowsweet	Star Anise
Chamomile	Henbane	Myrrh	Willow
Cypress	Hyacinth	Orris Root	Yarrow

The use of herbs adds potency to spellwork because they encompass all of the Elementals: Earth with their roots, leaves, flowers, nuts, and berries; Air with their fragrance; Fire with their growth from sunlight and their internally affecting qualities; and Water in their growth, juices, and nourishment. Herbs are selected in spellwork for the changes they are perceived to produce, or for the qualities they possess, represent, or relate to. When you add herbs to your work, you are increasing the connection between the Elementals and the spell, as well as enhancing the connection between the Elementals and yourself. The four qualities vibrate within you and the herbs, and are focused to work in the spell by your invoking of those powers through the characteristic of the herb, directed to a specific goal as described within the framework of the spell.

Daily Colors and Herbs

When creating spells, the days of the week can be used to enhance the power or direction of the spell. More strength can be added by attuning the day of the week with the herbs that relate to that particular day. Picking a color, as well as herbs, to match the day and planning your spells to take place on an appropriate day increases the power of the spell. You can fine tune it even more with day and night hours (based on sunrise and sunset) and their planetary aspects.

Monday: Silver, light gray, white
           Myrtle, violet, willow, wormwood

Tuesday: Red, orange
           Dragon's blood, patchouli

Wednesday: Violet, opal, iridescent, medium gray
Jasmine, lavender

Thursday: Blue, indigo, purple
Cinnamon, musk, nutmeg, sage

Friday: Green, aqua, lime
Saffron, sandalwood

Saturday: Black, dark gray, indigo
Black poppy seeds, myrrh

Sunday: Gold, orange, yellow, white
Frankincense, lemon

The best days for dark power spells are those of the Dark Sabbats, Dark Esbats, and celestial events such as eclipses and comet visits. Otherwise, the days most suitable for dark power magics are Saturday, Wednesday, and Monday. Although some names for the days of the week derive from such deities as Saturn, Woden, Thor, and Tiws (Northern version of war god, Mars), it was the positioning of the days in the week that held significance to my mother and grandmother. The first day of the week was considered to be Saturday, as is still seen in calendars from Spain, and sacred to the divine as Holly King, Ancient of Days, and Dark Lord. Wednesday is sacred to Annis, the Hag, Crone, and the Dark Lady. Monday is the Moon's Day and is excellent for Fairy magics, contacting the Sidhe, and working with Otherworld.

Dark Power Beverages and Foods

Certain foods and drinks are also associated with the dark energies. Blackberries are traditionally a Lughnassadh food, and usually made into pies and wine, to honor the god on entering the Underworld to begin his rule there as Lord of Shadows. Blackberry vines are sacred to both Hecate, who is called the goddess of the witches, and to Hades, the god of the Underworld (Roman name: Pluto).

Fruitcake, the traditional staple of Yuletide (and to some a flavorless concoction—I am including here my own recipe, which people assure me produces a wonderfully edible fruit cake), contains citron and other candied confections that represent the sun held still in the darkness, yet about to emerge after the solstice. Plum puddings (recipe to follow) use black currants and black raisins, the dried grapes of summer, to show the passage of the god from the Underworld and rebirth of the sun.

Dark breads such as rye, black, and pumpernickel breads are excellent for dark power rituals and are also good for offerings to the dead and to the dark aspects of the Divine. Cornbread and corn muffins specifically relate to the celebration of Lughnassadh. The addition of nuts to dark breads bring the focus to the god in the dark months of September, October, November, and December. For the dark goddess, the primary foods that my family has used to relate to her are apples, anise, cranberries, currants, and pomegranates. These can be put into recipes for pies, breads, and muffins.

Various drinks relate to the dark powers and can be used in rituals, spells, offerings, and meditations. Blackberry wine has already been mentioned; also suitable are creme de cassis (black currant) liqueur, and Opal Nera (made with anise and cassis). For nonalcoholic beverages, you could choose from apple juice, blackberry juice, grape juice, and tomato juice (tomatoes are related to the dark power herb belladonna). Elderberry wine is a rare find, and is perfect for an offering to the dark goddess or as a drink during a Dark Esbat or Lunar Eclipse ritual.

Edible Fruitcake

If you do not like some of the nuts or fruits called for in this recipe, then simply eliminate them. The recipe makes 2 large loaf-cakes.

2½	cups sifted flour	8	oz. chopped pecans
1	teaspoon baking soda	8	oz. chopped almonds
2	eggs, lightly beaten	8	oz. chopped hazelnuts
2⅔	cups mincemeat (28 oz. jar)	10	oz. chopped dates
1	14 oz. can sweetened condensed milk	6½	oz. candied cherries
		8	oz. candied pineapples
2	cups chopped walnuts	8	oz. candied citron

Butter a 9-inch tube pan (or two bread pans), line with wax paper, then butter again. Sift flour and soda in one bowl. In an extra large bowl, combine eggs, mincemeat, condensed milk, fruit, and nuts (this can be done by hand with a large wooden spoon). Fold in the flour and soda. Pour into two tube pans and bake in preheated, slow oven (300 degrees) for 1½ hours. Turn oven down to 275 degrees and continue to bake for another half-hour. The top will get brown, and your home will smell wonderful. Set fruitcakes on wire rack, turn out of pans and remove the wax paper. Enjoy!

Poppyseed and Wine Cake

This very simple recipe requires a bundt pan for the best results, but you can also use a tube pan. Good for Dark Esbats and Eclipses.

1	package yellow cake mix	¼	cup sherry
1	package vanilla instant pudding	¼	cup light cooking oil
		1	teaspoon nutmeg
4	eggs	2	tablespoons poppy seeds

Combine all ingredients in large bowl and beat for 5 minutes (by hand or in a mixer). Pour into a tube or bundt pan, and bake in preheated oven at 350 degrees for 45 minutes. Cool on rack, turn out, and leave plain, or sprinkle with confectionary sugar, or drizzle with icing (you can find poppy seed in the spice rack at most grocery stores).

Plum Pudding

To make this recipe, you will need to have a pressure cooker or means of achieving the same results without one. You will also need a pudding pan with a snap-on, or latched, lid.

1	cup raisins	½	teaspoon salt
2	cups currants	2	teaspoons cinnamon
¾	cup cut up citron	¾	teaspoon mace
½	cup candied lemon peel	½	teaspoon nutmeg
½	cup candied orange peel	¼	teaspoon ground cloves
½	cup finely chopped walnuts	½	pound finely chopped suet
1½	cups soft bread crumbs		(2 cups or 5 oz.)
	(4 slices of bread)	1	cup brown sugar (packed)
¼	cup cognac	3	eggs, beaten
1	cup flour	½	teaspoon vanilla extract
1	teaspoon baking soda	½	to 1 cup dark corn syrup

In a large bowl, toss the raisins, currants, citron, and candied peels with the cognac and let sit for 1 to 3 hours. If nonalcoholic plum pudding is desired, simply combine these ingredients without the cognac. Some people prefer brandy, whiskey, or rye flavored with rock sugar candy ("Rock and Rye").

After ingredients have marinated, in another large bowl, mix together flour, soda, walnuts, and seasonings. Add suet and brown sugar. (Suet is the white fat from along the spine of the beef animal; most grocery stores will charge only a few cents for this.) Mix well by hand, using your fingers to blend the suet. Add the marinated fruits and combine well.

In a separate bowl, combine eggs, syrup, and vanilla. Add bread crumbs and mix well. Stir this into the batter.

Grease pudding mold well. Pour in batter, leaving room for expansion, and snap cover closed. Place on rack in pressure cooker with 3 to 4 cups water. Cover cooker, leaving safety control valve open. Steam for 15 minutes, then close valve and cook for 1 hour at 15 pounds pressure (I watch this process for the whole hour, while doing dishes or whatever, to monitor the heat of the range, adjusting the temperature of the stove burner to keep the pressure at 15 pounds). Release steam all at once. Remove mold pan from cooker (it is *hot*), uncover, cool, turn over onto serving platter and remove mold. I like to decorate the pudding with artificial holly and leaves, but you can be quite creative in your presentation of this delicious Yule tradition.

Anise Tea Cakes

This is fine for a Dark Esbat treat. Makes 24 miniature muffins.

1	large egg (at room temperature)	½	teaspoons grated lemon rind
2	tablespoons sugar	¼	teaspoon crushed anise seeds
¼	cup flour		
2	tablespoons melted, cooled butter (or margarine)	⅛	teaspoon anise extract

In regular size mixer bowl, beat egg, extract, and sugar at high speed about 3 to 5 minutes until thick, pale yellow, and tripled in volume. By hand, quickly fold in flour, margarine, lemon rind, and anise seeds, being careful not to deflate the egg mixture. Spoon batter into greased miniature muffin pans. Bake in preheated oven at 350 degrees for 12 minutes, then cool on racks before turning out of the pans.

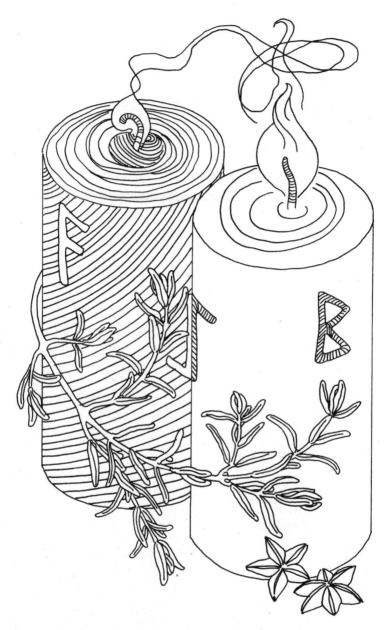

The nature of mind energy allows it to flow from within the body to the outside to effect changes in the real world. Much of what exists is first imagined, then brought into being by the deliberate actions of the ones who imagined, such as in the case of inventions.

— Spell —
Dark Power Exorcism:
Dark Power Ritual for Renewal of the Earth

Create the ritual circle; call upon the Elementals, greet the Lady and the Lord, then move into the following work. When the exorcism is completed, invoke the blessing of the Lady and the Lord with a ritual meal (Cakes and Wine), farewell the Elementals, and open the circle.

This ritual may be used to direct the dark power of chaos energy into the regeneration of the Earth and into opening the awareness of humanity to the need for balance and unity with our world. The nature of mind energy allows it to flow from within the body to the outside to effect changes in the real world. Much of what exists is first imagined, then brought into being by the deliberate actions of the ones who imagined, such as in the case of inventions. Likewise, think-groups meet to invent solutions and alternative approaches to various problems facing humanity and the planet today. By having a number of people looking at a problem, more ideas are generated to be discussed and enlarged upon to reach a common goal. Change the ritual as you feel is appropriate, because by putting something new into another person's ritual, you enhance it with your own creativity.

Begin with a soothing bath, casting a circle, and calling upon the Elementals. The timing of the ritual should coincide with the New Moon to emphasize a new beginning coming out of darkness into a new light, and the work area should face North, the realm of the Dark Lady and the Dark Lord.

Have in your circle sandalwood or patchouli oil for the dark powers; a container with ground cloves (or a whole clove) for protection and exorcism, cumin for exorcism, rosemary for exorcism and healing, a bay leaf for purification and healing, and anise (or a whole star anise) for purification and protection; a black pillar or votive candle and a matching white candle, each in a safe container that will hold the melted wax. Other herbs that can be used instead of the kitchen herbs are mullein for protection and exorcism, yarrow for exorcism, nettle for exorcism and healing, vervain for purification and healing, and burdock for purification and protection.

149

After the circle is cast and the Elementals called upon, rub the oil on the black and white candles, from the base to the top and envision the candles as being empowered by the Dark Lord and the Dark Lady respectively. You may want to state aloud that each is being consecrated to the appropriate deity.

Next, as you state aloud the meanings, inscribe around the black candle the runes for magical power: (As ᚨ), destruction (Haegal ᚾ), overcoming resistance (Thorn ᚦ), protection (Elhaz ᛉ), questing (Rad ᚱ), and channel (Eoh ᛇ). On the white candle state aloud the meanings and inscribe the runes for channel (Eoh ᛇ), healing (Sigel ᛋ), victory (Tyr ᛏ), new starts (Beorc ᛒ), and favorable outcome/ harvest (Ger ᛄ).

Hold up the unlit black candle and say:

> *Great Lord of Shadows, Leader of the Wild Hunt, Willing Sacrifice of Lughnassadh, I call upon thee with this thy candle! Bring to it the power of your destructive forces and the chaos of untamed energy under the guidance of the Elementals and with thy own protection.*

Set the candle in its fireproof container.

Move your wand slowly in a circular motion over the top of the candle counterclockwise as you say:

> *Bring to me the wrongs of the world; bring to me the sorrows. Bring to me the pain of the Earth; bring to me the fears of tomorrow. Here in this candle I direct the flow; here in this candle the chaos will go. Here in this candle the endings are sent; here in this candle the chaos is spent.*

Set down the wand and light the black candle. Hold up the white pillar candle and say:

> *Great Lady of Darkness, Crone of the Tomb, Lady of Discord, I call upon thee with this thy candle! Bring to it the power of your transformative forces and the rebirth of energy into new forms under the guidance of the Elementals and with thy own protection.*

Set the candle in its fireproof container.

Move your wand slowly in a circular motion over the top of the candle three times clockwise (and note to yourself the significance of moving in the opposite direction; of turning things around) as you say:

Heal thou the wrongs of the world; wipe away sorrows. Heal thou the pain of the Earth; brush away fears of tomorrow. Here in this candle the energy flows; here in this candle new forms are engendered. Here in this candle new beginnings evolve; here in this candle is chaos resolved.

Set down the wand and light the white candle.

With your knife or your fingers, take the clove (mullein), cumin (yarrow), and half of the rosemary (nettle) and drop each one in that order into the black candle and say:

These are the old forms of Chaos absorbed by the flame and purified by fire.

Envision the troublesome aspects of the world in the flame, and add more herbs, if you need, with additional envisioning of war, famine, disease, hatred, envy, environmental destruction, and pollution of the land, rivers, sea, and air. See these being consumed in the hungry flame of destruction. See the Wild Hunt gathering these hurts together.

Now take and drop into the flame of the white candle the rest of the rosemary (nettle) and see this crossover herb as channeling the energy of the black candle into the white candle, then add the bay (vervain) and anise (burdock), in that order, to the flame and say:

These are the Chaos forms transformed through the healing power of the Crone and brought into the Light.

Snuff out the black candle, but let the white candle burn for an hour, and while it burns, envision people at peace; children playing in a meadow; grains, vegetables, and fruit trees growing to produce a bountiful harvest; the world's forests regenerating; the waters of the Earth running pure and clean; and the air clear and bright. After an hour, snuff out the white candle to be set aside for later use.

Raise up your open arms to the Lady and the Lord and say:

Great Lady of Darkness and Light, Great Lord of Darkness and Light, together you dance the spiral of life, death, and rebirth in our hearts, our lives, and our world, yet we are one with thee and thee with me. Let the dance move to renewal and let thy great peace descend upon us and transform us that we may thrive in love for one another. So Mote It Be!

Lower your arms and say:

My blessings take with thee and thine come upon me. The ritual is ended; the circle is cleared.

Open the circle and ground the residual energy.
Take the black candle and bury it in the ground, saying:

Back to the dark cauldron, into the bower, let the Darkness this candle devour.

Light the white candle for world peace and cleansing whenever you feel the need until the candle is gone. You may repeat the ritual as often as you like.

In meditation, harnessing the power of the dark aspect of the Divine may be achieved in a variety of ways. For example, to focus on the renewal of the Earth, bring back to mind the Wild Hunt, but instead of harvesting the spirits of the dead, let the Rade collect the destructive thought patterns of the selfish and the vengeful. The Hunt can then take these to the Crone to be redirected and reborn as constructive to life on Earth.

When the Destroyer is directed toward releasing us from self-imposed bondage that drains our true spiritual energy, we will ride with the Wild Hunt, overturning outdated perceptions through enlightenment, and ushering in the optimistic change of the Lord of Shadows through the transformative power of the Dark Lady. This moves us into new opportunities and new inspiration—the Star of the Tarot applied to the development of humanity.

8

How Are Stones and Crystals Used?

A Word About Witch Tools

People write to me with questions about magical practices and the tools to carry out rituals and spells. They ask me how to get an athame or a wand, how to practice the Craft without their family finding out, and how to be practicing witches when they cannot find, afford, or keep tools. The stones and crystals listed here are tools of the Craft that may be found in your own back yard or local area, or may be obtained in rock shops and mail order catalogs (a few examples of the latter are listed at the end of this book). Not all tools have to look occult to be perfectly useful in the Craft.

When I was thirteen, I acquired my first athame (ritual knife)—it was actually a letter opener fashioned to look like a sword. Prior to that, I had used a simple, single-blade pocket knife. Both of these were tools that I kept with my personal things, carried on trips, and used to inscribe candles, stir herbs, and so forth, so these items had my energies in them. The point is that any knife or knife-like object can be your ritual athame. My early wands were simply sticks. Anyone can pick up a stick and have a wand, but it is the charging and use of that stick, the infusion of your own energy to work with that of the wood, that makes it a wand.

As time passed, I acquired a very nice ritual athame, a straight-bladed bolline, and a curve-bladed bolline, but I still use the letter opener from time to time, because it holds the past connected to the present. The little sword still contains the energy of my youth and reminds me to keep my awarenesses open.

Wands are another matter. I have several for different types of magical focus. Some of these wands I have selected from trees and cut with rituals of my own fashioning. Others I have *found* when I had need for a wand for an impromptu bit of magic work. My wands include a beautifully fashioned one of oak, a plain one of willow, and natural ones of elder, hazel, and hawthorn.

A stang is a perfect altar for beginners or those who want to practice without attracting attention to themselves around their families. This is a staff of wood—an inch or two thick is plenty large enough around, and a height of six feet is all you need—that can be straight or forked. Mine has three prongs, which I identify as representing to me the Threefold aspect of both the Lady and the Lord. You can decorate a stang with runes, or wrap it in yarns, leave it plain, or whatever. Set it where you want to face for your rituals, and it becomes the altar. Hang a wreath of flowers or vines on it for a Sabbat, artificial cobwebs for Samhain or Dark Moon rituals, and so forth—let your imagination play, for *play*, with the visualizations and empathic energy it generates, *is the stuff of magic.*

You do not have to own special tools to be a witch. A witch can pick up tools as needed from the surroundings. A stick, a rock, a shell, a kitchen knife—all these are equally fine tools for the inconspicuous witch. What is important is that you feel yourself connected with Nature, with the trees, the plants, the animals, fish, insects, and with the stars of the night sky.

The following list of stones and crystals will give you a means of focusing your energy through the magnifying power of these items. Meditation is one of the most power-inducing magical techniques for the witch, and these stones and crystals enhance that power, focus it, and direct it to the objective or goal desired by the witch. Other tools can be used for meditation, as already mentioned. Black mirrors, crystal balls, polished obsidian, and a variety of crystal stones all work well for meditation, travel to other worlds and planes, spiritual development, and transference of energy.

Gem and stone elixers are included, designated by an asterisk, with their general uses described in parenthesis. They can also be used in spellwork as energy-charged waters. To make an elixer, soak a charged gem/stone in a cup of spring water for an hour during a Full Moon or Dark Moon, depending on the purpose of the elixer. Then consecrate and store it away from light, drinking the elixer as needed. You may want to add a drop of whiskey or brandy to hold the energies.

Some stones and crystals have multiple styles and are listed in the general characteristic, then by color or type.

Magical Stones and Crystals

Agate: health; good fortune; eloquence; improves vitality, energy, self-confidence; gives bursts of mental or physical energy; balance emotions; calms body, mind, and emotions
  Banded: relieves stress
  White with **Blue/Black Spots**: travel
  Eye Formation: bodily protection; travel
  Mossy: healing; cleanses; strengthens; abundance; self-confidence; harmony; releases anger/frustration; connects with natural energies of the earth
  Milky with **Red**: visualizes; gains goals
Alexandrite: balances the nervous system; used in color therapy

Amazonite: good fortune; female power; soothes nervous system; improves thought process; regulates metabolism (sociability)

Amber: strengthens or breaks spells (thus a "witch's stone"); increases; success; health; healing; love; absorbs negative energies; manifestation; good luck (relief from despair)

Amethyst: spirituality; protects from negativity by transforming it; increases intuition; aids dreams; relieves tension; aids meditation; cleanses and energizes; protects against psychic manipulation (help in compromise)

Apache Tear: protects from evil of others; "grounding" own energies; spiritual meditation

Apatite: strengthens muscles and coordination

Aqua-Aura: meditation; release of emotional tension

Aquamarine: psychological influence; inspires the thought process; good luck in examinations, tests, or interviews (calms; relieves tension)

Auricalcite: calming; clears away tensions; neutralizes anger

Aventurine: creativity; luck in physical activities; courage; calming; aids sleep; leadership; decision-making (a wash to soothe the eyes; gains an open mind; curbs pride/aloofness)

Azurite (blended blues and greens): powerful psychic development; meditation; faces subconscious fears; healing; visions (help in controlling own reality)

Beryl: intellect; will-power; aids heart and digestive system (build self-esteem)

Bloodstone (Heliotrope): removes obstacles; vitality; enhances talents; balance chakras; protects good health; aids healing; wards injury; purifies the blood; courage; strength; integrity in relationships (curb obsessive affection)

Blue-Lace Agate: calms; frees self-expression; neutralizes anger; activates third eye; cleanses mental clutter and spiritual static (encourages trust and friendliness)

Blue Quartz: releases emotional tension; soothes

Boji Stone: strengthens chakras; healing; regenerates; balances body's energy fields (use as paired stones— one is smooth while the other is bumpy with projections)

Calcite (Gold): healing; cheerfulness (helps to reach for new goals and emotional contacts)

Calcite (Green): soothes fears; calming; aids intuition; transitions

Calcite (Orange): physical energy; expands awareness; intuition

Carnelian: career success; fast action; shielding thoughts; aids for good health; protection; "grounding" energy; motivates; energizes personal power

Chalcedony: optimism; spiritual/artistic creativity

Chalcopyrite (Peacock Stone): alleviates worry; aids focus for prosperity; happiness; protects from negativity

Chrysocolla: balance; cleanses negativity; contentment; healing; good luck; prosperity; clears mind (open a path away from daily routine)

Chrysoprase: peace; meditation; clairvoyance; gains incentive (tempers egotism)

Citrine: success; clarity of thoughts; protection; direction; induces dreams; improves self-image/confidence; prosperity; manifests personal power; initiative; creativity; endurance

Coral: calms; relaxes; protects from illness; wards evil thoughts of others

Diamond: protection; avert unseen dangers; emotional healer; power; purity; strength

Dioptase: relaxation; relieve stress; overcome emotional loss

Dolomite: averts fear of failure (focus on success; gain resourcefulness)

Emerald: artistic talent; memory; truth; visions; business success; peace; love; psychic insight; tranquility

Flourite: meditation; Fairy Realms; dreams; past lives; aids intellect; heals energy drains in the aura; helps to ground, balance, and focus energy; absorbs and alters negative energy; discernment; aids concentration

Garnet: swift movement; balances energies; revitalization; aids self-esteem and self-confidence; dreamwork; energy and courage; love and bonding; devotion

Geodes: freedom of spirit; linking with the cosmic dance

Hemitite: communication skills; enhances astral projection; balance and focus of energy; clear, calm reasoning; draws good relationships (diminishes defenselessness)

Herkimer Diamond: relieves stress; power booster for crystals/bojis; dream interpretation; psychic attunement (to gain goals; freer expression of love)

Iron Pyrite: attract success; health, wealth, and happiness; intellect; creativity; psychic development; channeling; memory

Jacinth: spiritual insight

Jade: peace; cleansing; harmony; friendship; good luck; protection; safe travel; wisdom; long life; dream focus/content (making ideals more realistic and practical)

Jasper: strengthen energy flow; relieve stress; gather energy for directing; nurturing; protection; grounding; safe astral travel
    Red: returns negativity to sender; defensive magics
    Brown: grounding and stability; soothes nerves
    Green: healing and fertility

Jet: binding (thus another "witch's stone," seen in jet and amber necklaces); calms fears; protection

Kunzite: meditation; balances negative emotions; purification; connection with the Divine

Kyanite: meditation; past lives recall; channeling; vivid dreams; enhances visualizations; altered states; serenity; manifestation of thought into reality

Lapis Lazuli: authority; power booster; aura cleanser; aids psychic development; mental balance; self-awareness; inner truths and wisdom; access universal knowledge

Larimar: transmutes negative energies like anger, greed, and frustration; brings excessive energies into balance

Lazurite: visions

Magnetite (Howlite): meditation; tranquility; calmness; honesty; aids against fear and anger

Malachite: business success; protection; vision quest; meditation; prosperity; hope; health; happiness; averts confusion and apathy; manifestation of desires (eases focus for controlling reality)

Moldavite: meteorite stone; transformations; star communication; heals longings; aids in finding true purpose in life; dimensional travel (aids in decision making; gaining confidence; re-focusing)

Moonstone: enhances psychic abilities; divination; love; comfort; peacefulness; long life; friendships; inspiration; draws attachments and sensitivity to wearer; wish granting; new beginnings (to feel at ease in one's surroundings; curb spending)

Morion Crystal: nearly black crystal used for grounding energies

Obsidian: protection; scrying; Dark Aspect meditation; Otherworld contact; Shadowland contact; banish grief; benevolence; healing

Obsidian Snowflake: grounding; responsibility; purification; changes; growth; deflect negative energy

Onyx: equilibrium; end worry; encourage justice; aids concentration and devotion; guidance through dreams and meditation; balance of duality (Black: deal with emotions/frustration)

Opal: psychic power; astral travel; meditation; calms; directs thoughts inward; reflects back to the wearer what is sent out; shape-shifting; invisibility (relaxation; calmative)

Pearl: astral projection; dreams (eases fears; calms the nerves)

Peridot: soulmates; clairvoyance; solar power; attracts occult power; inner vision; opens awareness; wards negativity; body tonic

Petrified Wood: meditation for past lives recall; physical energy; serenity; balance; grounding; vitality

Pumice: power; manifestation

Quartz Crystal: psychic power; vision quest; protection; energy; divination; projection; attaining goals; cleanse auras; meditation; intuitive thinking; store, focus, direct, transmit energy (protection). NOTE: to "program" a crystal, hold it to the third eye and focus on what purpose the crystal should be used for.

Quartz (Rose): peace; love; comfort; companionship (self-discipline; responsibility)

Quartz (Rutilated): increases strength of will (control self-indulgence)

Quartz (Smokey): generate energy; protection; purifies energies; Fairy connection; disperse negativity and draw positive energies (enhance interaction with others)

Quartz (Snow): meditation; serenity; peace; contemplation

Rhodochrosite: generate energy; physical and emotional balance; heals trauma; union of male and female aspects (regain emotional energy after frustrations)

Rhodinite: self-esteem; physical energy; self-actualization; service (eases physical fatigue; negating fear of criticism)

Rock Crystal: scrying; energizing; water magics

Ruby: protects health and wealth; contentment; increases energy and creativity; aids self-confidence, intuition, and courage; spiritual wisdom; generates heat

Sapphire: wisdom; material gains; attracts good influences; peace of mind; instills hope

Sardonyx: draw troubles then toss into the sea; self-protection

Selenite: calming for meditation and visualization; clarifies thoughts; healing (overcome guilt; letting go of negativity; curb overactive fantasizing)

Sodalite: meditation; enhances memory; relieves stress; aids sleep; enhances logical thought; stimulates intellect (control rage; curb need for negative attention)

Staurolite (Fairy Cross): good luck; protection; security; manifesting higher self on earth plane; astral connection; confidence

Sugilite: logic; business expertise; astral travel; manifestation; self-healing

Sunstone: energy; healing; success

Tiger Eye: good luck; objectivity; truth; self-confidence; protection from ill will of others; harmony; grounding; stability; instinctive and psychic ability; wisdom; healing (builds self-confidence)

Topaz (Blue): psychic insight; spiritual growth; leadership; concentration; clarity of thought

Topaz (Yellow): stress; deep sleep; psychic ability; calms body and mind; fulfillment of dreams and wishes by focusing into the facets; intentional creation; healing; attracts prosperity; communicates with other realms; revitalizes bodily energies (commitment to action; building willpower and decisiveness)

Tourmaline (Blue): clear speech; unblocks mind and emotions (rub to generate electrical charge to direct energy)

Tourmaline (General): beauty; freshness; joy; friendships; grounding; protection; calmness; self-confidence; attract goodwill; inspiration; discernment

Tourmaline (Green/Black): prosperity; deflects negative energies
(**Black:** redirects restlessness into productivity)
(**Green:** setting reasonable goals)

Tourmaline (Watermelon/Pink): self understanding
(**Pink:** encourages creativity; frees the personality)
(**Watermelon:** encouraging practical approach to making ideas real)

Turquoise: verbal communication; putting thoughts into words with ease; protection of the spirit; health; love; joy; social life; meditation; intuition; unification of spiritual and physical (open awareness to find creative solutions to problems; curbs fear of the dark)

Unikite: grounding; balance; stability

Vivianite (Rare): rebirth; clear sightedness; enlightenment

Zircon: spiritual sight; spiritual understanding

These stones and crystals can be used in spellwork. They can be infused with the magical intent, consecrated and dropped into candle magics, wrapped into a sachet, added to a dream pillow, or placed with the spell materials when buried. If used in candle magics, the stone may be used repeatedly simply by removing it from the wax when you are finished, washing it, and cleansing it again with the power of the Elementals. Store it in a dark cloth or away from light so it can re-gather its energies.

Place your stones in the light of the Full Moon or other cosmic entity for energizing. Dark Moon energizing is good for obsidian and other dark power stones. Eclipses help to energize stones for passage between the worlds.

Recent comets have been excellent occasions for energizing crystals, especially with the focus on the ancientness of the comet, its lonely travels lighting a glimmering path through the vast darkness of space, the changes incurred on the worlds it has passed once before, and the feeling of agedness, timelessness, and eternity such wonders bring to the senses.

161

With crystal gazing (not with a crystal ball, which is best in a footed holder), hold the stone in the palm of your hand and examine it while sitting comfortably. Look for the inner facets of refracting light and see if images form for you. When you spot something within the crystal, focus on it. Open your awareness to receive what lies within. You are connected with the Divine and with all of Nature, so there is nothing to fear in this. This is perhaps one of the major differences between Green Witchcraft and ceremonial magics—the practitioner neither fears nor seeks to dominate but is seen instead as co-existing in Nature and the Universe.

If your crystal takes you on a journey into the Underworld, you are learning to connect with the dark powers and see these powers for the wholeness they offer you. Being in balance with the dark and the light means invoking in your magical workings that essential of witchcraft: *with perfect love and perfect trust.*

When gazing into the crystal, do not let your vision blur. Instead, pick a light within the crystal to focus on, and keep it in focus. You will find that you are entering the crystal, and the room around you will disappear. If you sit and observe this happening, making note to yourself of this sensation, you probably will not travel very far. But Nature is patient. Once you feel comfortable with the idea of travel, you can relax and let the room disappear with little notice as you remain focused on the journey itself. The key is relaxation.

To imbue a crystal with energies, you may want to keep one large stone as a *generator.* This one is consecrated at the Full Moon, with fresh water from a running stream if at all possible, or with spring water. It is refreshed with the Full Moon and allowed to sit in the moonlight for a few hours—window sills are fine for this—then put away. When you want to realign a stone or crystal you have used in a spell, you can charge it by placing the generator crystal on it, and placing both on a pentacle on your altar. An hour is sufficient for this.

Most spellwork and magical workings require an hour at most to "percolate" for the effect desired. When you are done with your magics, remember to ground yourself by touching the floor or earth with the palms of your hands. Let that excess energy flow out so you are not jittery, then eat something and resume a normal routine.

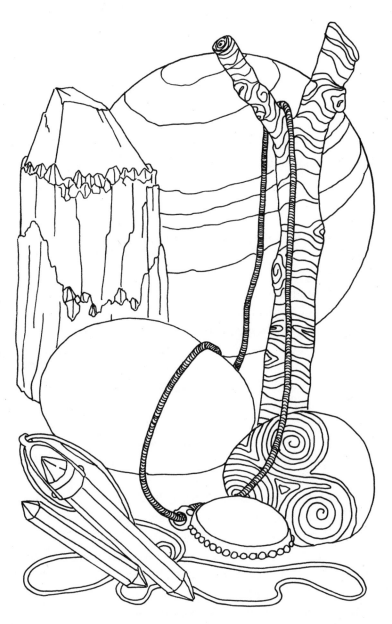

If your crystal takes you on a journey into the Underworld, you are learning to connect with the dark powers and see these powers for the wholeness they offer you. Being in balance with the dark and the light means invoking in your magical workings that essential of witchcraft: with perfect love and perfect trust.

— Rituals —
Dedication and Re-dedication
of Crystals and Stones

A number of crystals and stones benefit from a ritual dedication. This is like programming the crystal so you should stick to that focus, using a different crystal for another focus. If you find that you cannot locate another crystal or want to change the empowerment of one, then you can cleanse and rededicate the one you have already programmed. Both examples are given here. Although I will be addressing crystals, these rituals can be applied to stones. Simply look up the qualities of the stone and dedicate it to an appropriate focus.

Many crystals are dedicated during the Full Moon, but if you want a dark power crystal, the dedication can be during the Dark Moon. The same crystal can be dedicated at both Esbats to give it a wide range of use and wholeness. Think about the purpose you want the crystal to serve when you consider the type of moon dedication you will use. Peace, love, healing, contentment, generating positive energy, cleansing, physical energy, and gaining goals tend to be Light Aspect powers. Psychic power, vision quest, divination, meditation, intuition, protection, material gains, exorcism, willpower, and spiritual energy tend to be Dark Aspect powers.

The Esbat ritual for the Dark Moon was described earlier with the consecrating of a dark power tool, and the Full and New Moon ritual is detailed in Green Witchcraft for consecrating a light power tool. Begin by sweeping the circle. White candles are set at the Quarters (North, East, South, and West) for a dedication at the Full Moon; black or dark purple candles for a dedication at the Dark Moon.

Use incense with a light aroma such as sandalwood for the Full Moon; a more pungent aroma, such as patchouli, for the Dark Moon, or burn mugwort for either. Place your usual items on the altar—matches, water, sea salt (or rock salt), a pentacle, cup of drink, bite to a eat (such as a cupcake, muffin, or bread), something to represent the God and the Goddess and a candle for each, a cauldron for your libations, knife, wand, an anointing oil, crystals to be dedicated, and a center votive candle of white or dark purple, depending on the Moon.

Cast your circle and call upon the Elementals to attend. Do the Libations of Greeting in which you call upon the Lady and the Lord to meet with you in the circle.

Consecration of a Crystal

Think about what focus you want your crystal to have (look at the sample list) and have that in mind before you begin the ritual.

Set the crystal on the pentacle. Take up the athame and hold it high, upright, in your right hand, touch the crystal with your left, and say:

> *I call upon the power of the Elementals and the Divine to this place which is not a place, in this time which is not a time, as I stand between the worlds at the temple of my circle to empower this crystal of earth and light* (or earth and darkness).

Remove your hand from the crystal and hold your ritual knife with both hands. Feel the power of the Lady and the Lord course into the blade of the athame, then lower the knife to touch the crystal with the tip of the blade and see the energy run through the knife and into the crystal.

> *By the Divine Power of the Universe, is this crystal now focused as one of* (state the focus: "cleansing").

Put the athame on the altar and pick up the crystal. Hold it to the place of your third eye (the spot between your eyes and above your nose at the center of your forehead). Concentrate on the purpose for which this crystal is dedicated and feel that energy enter into the crystal, and unite with the matrix of the crystal so that the stone recognizes your energy.

> *With me and through me do you work to* (state the focus: "cleansing"), *for we are connected one to the other through the Elementals, that we are kith and kin. So Mote It Be!*

165

Take the crystal away from your third eye and consecrate it through the Elementals by sprinkling it with blessed water and passing it through the incense, doing these steps while you say:

> *In the names of the Lady and Lord,* (names you use or no names, only Lady and Lord) *I consecrate this crystal to be used in my practice of the Craft for* (state the focus). *I charge that this be so, and empower this crystal through Elemental Earth and Elemental Water* (sprinkle with salted water); *through Elemental Fire and Elemental Air* (pass through the incense smoke). *By the power of the Elementals is this crystal focused to aid me in my work. So Mote It Be!*

Set the crystal back on the pentacle and say:

> *Great Lady and Great Lord, together in the* (light or darkness) *of this Moon, you dwell within all. You are beginnings, fullness, and endings that lead into the cycle anew. You are the Energy of Life, Love Manifested and the Promise Fulfilled. Imbue this crystal with your power and love to aid me in my Craft.*

Hold the crystal above the votive candle and say:

> *Let this small light represent the power of the Moon and the Sun, illuminating and energizing this crystal to focus on* (name the focus) *for my use in my Craft.*

For a Light Power Crystal
Then with the crystal in your right hand, hold it aloft, and with your left hand held so your palm is against your heart, say:

> *Let me always remember the Rules of Conduct that I harm none in the practice of my Craft, for what is sent comes back. I work with the powers of the Goddess and the God with perfect love and perfect trust. By your power is this crystal charged, imbued, and dedicated to my Craft.*

Envision the light energy coming from your heart, passing into the left palm, traveling through the left arm, across the shoulders, into the right arm, up the right arm, into the right hand, and filling the upraised crystal.

For a Dark Power Crystal

Then with the crystal in your right hand, hold it aloft, and with your left hand held so your palm is parallel to the ground, say:

> *Lord of Shadows hidden within the Lady of Darkness, together they hold the darkness in Balance. He is the passing, she is the passage, together they move from life into life. With my hand in theirs, I call upon them to share their presence with me and pass dark power into this crystal that it may be charged, imbued, and dedicated to my Craft.*

Envision the dark energy shooting up from the ground, into the palm of the left hand, traveling through the left arm, across the shoulders into the right arm, up the right arm into the right hand, and into the tool.

Dedication of the Crystal Continues

Set the crystal back on top of the pentacle and kneel so that both palms now rest on the ground and say:

> *As what is sent returns, so I return to my Lady and my Lord the power so graciously sent to me. My crystal is sanctified through thy power and grace, attuned to me by passage through my flesh and my blood, and is ready for my use. So Mote It Be!*

Stand and remove the tool from the pentacle, but keep it on the altar; snuff the votive candle and say:

> *The energies borrowed are returned, yet remain as part of the continuing cycle of life essence. The path between the worlds is closed, yet remains open to my heart and to my Craft as I have need.*

The ritual ends with Cakes and Wine. Conclude with the blessings and the clearing of the circle, then Farewell the Elementals, open the circle, and put away your tools. The libation cauldron is poured into a depression in the ground and covered over (or a large flowerpot of soil can be used). The libation remains can also be simply washed down the sink while you envision it traveling through pipes and linkages back to the sea.

Crystal Rededication

Again, use one of the Esbat rituals as appropriate for dark or light power rededication. It is best to rededicate in the same power, with only the focus changing. If, however, you are taking a light power crystal and realigning it to dark power, or the other way around, optimum results will be obtained through using two rituals. During the Moon that matches the stone's current alignment, simply use the cleansing portion of the following ritual. Then dedicate the crystal anew during the Moon proper for the desired focus.

Begin by sweeping the circle. White candles are set at the Quarters (North, East, South, and West) for a dedication at the Full Moon, and black or dark purple candles for a dedication at the Dark Moon.

Use a cleansing incense such as frankincense or lavender (refer to the list in Chapter 7), or burn a suitable herb such as clove or burdock (see list and pick what you feel works best for you). Place your usual items on the altar—matches, water, sea salt (or rock salt), a pentacle, cup of drink, a bite to eat (such as a cupcake, muffin, or bread), something to represent the God and the Goddess and a candle for each, a cauldron for your libations, knife, wand, an anointing oil, crystals to be dedicated, and a center votive candle of white or dark purple, depending on the Moon.

In addition, you will need on your altar a small white or black (purple) cloth to wrap the crystal in for part of the ritual.

Place the crystal on top of the pentacle.

Cast your circle and call upon the Elementals to attend. Do the Libations of Greeting in which you call upon the Lady and the Lord to meet with you in the circle.

Take the crystal from the pentacle and hold it up in both hands to address the power of the Divine and say:

> *Behold this, the crystal I dedicated to* (previous focus), *but now I have another need. Harken unto the voice of your child, and see into my need. Like the seed that becomes new life in the womb of the Mother is this crystal placed into the cauldron of the Goddess. Let this crystal travel through the waters of life and into rebirth to be cleansed of my former need and brought forth to work with me in my Craft to a new focus.*

Place the crystal inside the cauldron (it will get wet from the libation already in there), and set the cauldron on top of the pentacle. Pour a bit of the blessed water over the crystal and say:

> *You are cleansed and purified in the cauldron of rebirth.*

Take the crystal out of the cauldron and set the cauldron back in its former place on the altar. Pass the crystal through the incense smoke and say:

> *By fire and air are you brought into new life.*

Envision the crystal as newly formed by geological fusions, birthed from the depths of the rocky earth, and pushed out of the ground through upheaval into the light. Wrap it in the cloth as a comforting swaddling, drying it off and then carefully unwrapping the crystal to see it as a shining new being.

Set the cloth aside and place the crystal on the pentacle. Take up the athame and hold it high, upright, in your right hand, touching the crystal with your left, and say:

> *I call upon the power of the Elementals and the Divine to this place which is not a place, in this time which is not a time, as I stand between the worlds at the temple of my circle to empower this crystal of earth and light* (or earth and darkness).

Remove your hand from the crystal and hold your ritual knife with both hands. Feel the power of the Lady and the Lord course into the blade of the athame, then lower the knife to touch the crystal with the tip of the blade and see the energy run through the knife and into the crystal.

> *By the Divine Power of the Universe, is this crystal now focused as one of* (new focus, for example: "meditation").

Put the athame on the altar and pick up the crystal. Hold it to the place of your third eye (the spot between your eyes and above your nose at the center of your forehead). Concentrate on the purpose for which this crystal is rededicated and feel that energy enter into the crystal, and unite with the matrix of the crystal so that the stone recognizes your energy.

> *With me and through me do you work to* (state focus: "aid meditation"), *for we are connected one to the other through the Elementals, that we are kith and kin. So Mote It Be!*

Take the crystal away from your third eye and reconsecrate it through the Elementals by sprinkling it with blessed water and passing it through the incense, and as you so this, say:

> *In the names of the Lady and Lord,* (names you use or no names, only Lady and Lord) *I consecrate this crystal to be used in my practice of the Craft for* (state the focus). *I charge that this be so, and empower this crystal through Elemental Earth and Elemental Water* (sprinkle with salted water); *through Elemental Fire and Elemental Air* (pass through the incense smoke). *By the power of the Elementals is this crystal focused to aid me in my work. So Mote It Be!*

Set the crystal back on the pentacle and say:

> *Great Lady and Great Lord, together in the* (light or darkness) *of this Moon, you dwell within all. You are beginnings, fullness, and endings that lead into the*

cycle anew. You are the Energy of Life, Love Manifested and the Promise Fulfilled. Imbue this crystal with your power and love to aid me in my Craft.

Hold the crystal above the votive candle and say:

Let this small light represent the power of the Moon and the Sun, illuminating and energizing this crystal to focus on (name the focus) *for my use in my Craft.*

For a Light Power Crystal

Then with the crystal in your right hand, hold it aloft, and with your left hand held so your palm is against your heart, say:

Let me always remember the rules of conduct that I harm none in the practice of my Craft, for what is sent comes back. I work with the powers of the Goddess and the God with perfect love and perfect trust. By your power is this crystal charged, imbued, and dedicated to my Craft.

Envision the light energy coming from your heart, passing into the left palm, traveling through the left arm, across the shoulders, into the right arm, up the right arm, into the right hand, and filling the upraised crystal.

For a Dark Power Crystal

Then with the crystal in your right hand, hold it aloft, and with your left hand held so your palm is parallel to the ground, say:

Lord of Shadows hidden within the Lady of Darkness, together they hold the darkness in balance. He is the passing, she is the passage, together they move from life into life. With my hand in theirs, I call upon them to share their presence with me and pass dark power into this crystal that it may be charged, imbued, and dedicated to my Craft.

Envision the dark energy shooting up from the ground, into the palm of the left hand, traveling through the left arm, across the shoulders into the right arm, up the right arm into the right hand, and into the tool. (Dedication of the crystal continues.)

Set the crystal back on top of the pentacle and kneel so that both palms now rest on the ground and say:

> *As what is sent returns, so I return to my Lady and my Lord the power so graciously sent to me. My crystal is sanctified through thy power and grace, attuned to me by passage through my flesh and my blood, and is ready for my use. So Mote It Be!*

Stand and remove the tool from the pentacle, but keep it on the altar; snuff the votive candle and say:

> *The energies borrowed are returned, yet remain as part of the continuing cycle of life essence. The path between the worlds is closed, yet remains open to my heart and to my Craft as I have need.*

The ritual ends with Cakes and Wine. Conclude with the blessings and the clearing of the circle, then Farewell the Elementals, open the circle, and put away your tools. The libation cauldron is emptied into a depression in the ground and covered over (or a large flowerpot of soil can be used). The libation remains can also be simply washed down the sink while you envision it traveling through pipes and linkages back to the sea.

9

What Are Green Witchcraft Meditations?

Uses of Meditations

Various types of meditations have been demonstrated throughout this book. The sequence of actions is basic, with the simple breathing exercise an easy entry to the meditative state, but there is more to this than simply an altered state of awareness. Many people use meditation to relax, to open their subconscious so fresh ideas can come into their conscious minds, and to refresh themselves during the hectic workday.

In Green Witchcraft, the primary use of meditation is to connect with the All—to be a fully cognizant partner in the functioning of

Nature and the Cosmos. There is more to the sequence of events than breathing. There is intent or purpose, focus, and connection. Up to a point, there is a correlation between witchcraft and shamanism in this meditative state, but the purpose is what generally makes the distinction between the two. Shamanism is primarily invoked to intercede in life-threatening situations such as illness. The purpose is to find the spirit of the person in need and either to guide that spirit to final rest or to a return to health. In the Green Craft, while the former may hold true in some cases, the usual purpose is that of union, identity, and communication.

Types of Meditations

The basic types of meditation are those of union, transposition, communication, travel, and any combination of these. Union with objects in Nature or with the creatures of Nature bring to your awareness your oneness with them. You see things from a different perspective and experience life from another's point of view. With transposition, you are projecting yourself into the other animal or object. This is a spiritual, or form of astral, extension of yourself so that you feel existence in the way that the object or being you have entered feels existence. You experience the being of another. Through communication, you express kinship and oneness with the creatures and objects of Nature. With travel, you move through the universe or through the planes of universe.

My favorite memories of childhood meditations involved the activity of becoming a variety of animals. Living the life-patterns of foxes, cats, dogs, horses, eagles, wolves, bears, and cougars was a natural experience for me. Envisionment meant assuming the characteristics of the animal, seeing through the creature's eyes and utilizing the creature's senses. Sniffing the air for the scents on the breeze and distinguishing what those scents are, moving with silent stealth, running with the easy smoothness of sure-footed limbs, nestling in appropriate habitat, and listening with alertness—all were actions played out with the energy of youthful exhuberance. No placid games for me! I like to think that the few friends I could muster to participate in these learning exercises came away with a special memory for their later years.

This is the first level of meditation that I experienced—acting the part of various animals and gaining an appreciation for the special gifts and qualities they possessed and offered. I watched my daughter sit in silent stillness on the grass in a park where rabbits abound and knew that she merged with them when they came to her unafraid. She later told me that she would think of herself as rabbit, and they sensed the connection. I saw and recognized the transition from child to animal because I had done it myself many times.

The next level of meditation takes you into a quiet place within yourself. This is not the same as the altered awareness of transcendental meditation or inner transformation meditation. Instead, the meditation is undertaken out-of-doors. There are a number of places for this kind of meditation, and it is easy to move into the awareness. Sit on a meadow hill, a mountain's peak, a woodland, a pasture, the back yard, or in the garden—these are all places where a person can merge with Nature.

Merging meditation involves seeing something, then transporting yourself into what it is that you are seeing, so that, in essence, you see yourself from a different perspective. This can be very startling to an animal, so move with care and kindly intent. Animals do not seem to mind a merging, as long as they perceive a kindred spirit. Watch a bird in flight, for example, then envision yourself moving upward quickly and into that bird's body, looking through that bird's eyes to see the ground far below, and yourself sitting in a chair in the corner of your garden. Leave the bird and return to your body, exhilarated by the flight. I leave the aerobatics to others!

Look at the cat licking her paw. Move yourself into her body and feel your rough tongue licking the short stiff hairs of the paw, the spread-out fingers of the paw with the claws extended so you can get at the hairs between. Think about the sensations you experience here. You have hair everywhere, and the midday sun is hot on your fur. What would you like right now? A cool slab of concrete to lay your belly on. Think about the garage door being open enough to let you pad silently inside, then withdraw back into your own body.

Does the cat trot off to the garage? Does the cat give you an odd look? Does the cat come to investigate you?

Cats are very intuitive and perceptive, so when you move into a cat, be aware you may be shut out or found newly intriguing. Dogs simply get a little nervous at the intrusion. Horses do not seem to mind, and wild animals tend to find the incursion fascinating. There seems to be quite a difference between the responses of wild and domesticated animals.

Not all meditations involve animals. There is the identification with rocks, boulders, mountains, streams, rivers, trees, forests, sandy beaches, and the sea. There are also the animals of the sea to identify with. Everything from crabs and clams, snuggling into the mud for safety, to jellyfish and stingrays rolling in the surf, can be blended with. My husband had a momentary response of "Wow!" once when we were leaving the coastal town where we had lived for two years, and I called out to the dolphins to bid me farewell. About a dozen of the beauties flew out of the sea in unison as we passed by on the bridge.

Curiously, there is also an advantage to the sensation of being unaware of danger. If you percieve of yourself as being secure in the presence of wild animals, for example, this can act as a dampener to any sense of aggression that the animal might ordinarily feel. If you feel threatened, or act threatened, the animal will pick up on that and respond to your fear, most likely by attacking. I have talked to wild foxes, who paced alongside me in the woods, then turned aside when I reassured them that I was not interested in finding their burrow and babies. I have greeted a solitary wolf staring at me while I hiked in the wilderness, and by his stance and the look in his eyes, I felt that we exchanged a sense of community before he trotted off into the woods. Later, I realized that I could have been in danger, but at the time, all I felt was calmness and the joy of oneness with nature.

Love of nature is all-inclusive—from the prickly starfish to the waddling skunk—but this does not mean I have actively gone out to confront a wild animal to prove connection. There is a fine difference between *living* life, and *creating* situations that force

176

encounters. Nature knows the difference. Do not go into the woods with the intent of proving a point; that infers smug superiority and prideful dominance. Nature loves to confound such notions. The Green Witch is at one with nature, not out to dominate nature. Acceptance of the connection, rather than the need for proof, is the tone preferred.

Communication meditation is another matter. This is a type of meditative state that is fleeting and exotic when it is sensed. No preparation is needed except the calm centeredness that comes from feeling at one with everything around you. Peacefulness and tranquility permeate your presence, and that is when communication takes place. Now is when your favorite pet speaks to you and you understand—the language barrier evaporates. This happens, too, when you suddenly realize that the speech on the news that you were listening to absently and understanding perfectly, is in a language you do not speak. The only problem with conscious realization is that the communication tends to end at that point. With a little practice at retaining that detatched sensation, the session will come to last longer.

Communication with rocks is not absurd nor unusual, especially if you have already been using crystals and stones in magical work. Sit next to a large boulder, put your arms around it, and lean into its sun-warmed hard surface, your face against it. Now look around yourself from this position and see what the stone has seen. The stone may tell you of having slid down from a greater height and being stopped by the outcrop of a tree root. It may tell you of storms that have crashed around it and the lightning that once struck it. You look to the other side of the stone and see the blackened mark on it, then lean onto it again. Stones are usually so surprised that someone has taken the time to visit with them that they can be quite eloquent and effusive. It is not mere coincidence that our ancestors made great monuments of standing stones, nor odd that they saw the wisdom of the ancient rocks they honored with water and flowers. Human history is beautifully evoked in the stones of the past, so that when we stand among them today, we feel strangely connected and we are awed by their testimony.

To experience cosmic travel, you have only to lie on your back at night and gaze upward at the stars. See the points of light in the sky and know that for the most part, the stars are either moved from there or not there at all, but it is their ancient light that you see. Project yourself outward and upward into the sky. Move through the atmosphere, past the thin clouds and into the realm of satellites, space shuttles, and orbiting space labs. I always liked the scene of the angel getting hit by a telecommunications satellite when on the way to earth to collect a soul ("Date With An Angel"), but you are not solid, and you can pass through any such interference as a vaporous light.

Moving higher into space, you see the planet of Earth recede, becoming the blue sphere with white swirls familiarized by the flights to the moon. Now you turn your vision away from the Earth and into the darkness of space, moving past the planets of the solar system, hearing the hydrogen roar of the Sun lessening as you travel outward. There is no up or down, there is no sense of direction except away from the Earth, and "away" stretches in all directions. The last lonely planet spins silently by, and you realize there are more than nine in our solar system. You suppress a smile at your newly acquired secret knowledge, which no one will accept for now, and continue your journey.

Meteors, comets, gaseous formations, the roar and thunder of new life coming into being on unknown worlds, the demise of life on other worlds comes to your ken—energy passing from one form and moving through space to re-emerge in another form, sensing you and being sensed by you in the passage. Ebb and flow of dark and light, the dust of alien worlds, the gaps in the surface of space rubble, the very light of the stars evaporating as you approach, to reveal the darkness where once they were, and the path to where they have moved. These paths, along with black holes and pulsars, all beckon to you.

You may want to plan your cosmic travels in advance so that you allow yourself plenty of time to explore. The first two or three trips give you a chance to map out areas that interest you most, then you know the most direct route to the site and can move swiftly to the place you want to explore.

With astral travel, however, the best time is when in a meditative state that is planned and perhaps done in a ritual circle. This type of journey is to other planes and worlds, with the most familiar being Underworld and Otherworld. The boundaries of these worlds are expansive and limited only by the itinerary of the traveler. Some examples of Otherworld and Underworld travel have already been given with the Companion Quest and the Passing the Midhes Spell.

A crystal ball is excellent for astral travel. The use of magical tools in meditation aid in the focus, but are not necessary for successful travel. They do, however, help set the mood and the atmosphere. The use of ritual programs the conscious mind to recognize it is time to let the subconscious mind come forward. Repetition of rituals makes the transition easier. The black mirror is also a fine tool for astral travel, and can move you to other worlds and other times.

If ever in your workings you become fearful, you need to examine the cause. Social and cultural heritages have a lot of fear ingrained, so that it may be necessary to retreat to your cave of the first meditation and seek out what it is that you fear, and why. When you imagine your worst fear and feel it overpowering you, you need to face that fear and move through the torment. Once you do this, you move into a different stage—one where the fear is already known and faced—and now it feels devoid of power over you. It may still be there, but you have unmasked it and neutralized it. This is a kind of dark passage through the Underworld, which allows you to call on the dark powers with greater understanding, and unites you in Wholeness.

Creative Meditations

Another type of meditation that is actually a combination of communication and astral connection is that of meditative writing and singing. Place yourself in a relaxed, meditative state, and let yourself go with pen in hand. Do not be surprised if you compose lyrical music to the Moon, with haunting melodies that become your offering to the Goddess, with words or sounds that come unbidden. This is a Craft version of speaking in tongues, and is incidentally one of the criticisms some Christian denominations have of the Pentacostal sects—it is too pagan. Remember the Oracle Cave meditation, and when you do it, your own words will come out.

Once you have experienced this type of astral communication, you can prepare for it and direct it to a specific purpose, such as poetry or creative writing. The expressions that you give voice to or write down are perhaps not of the flowery quality of literary publications, but these are impressions that come to you and have deep meaning to you. Insight can be called for, along with memory and an expression of connection when you invoke this kind of meditative interaction with the power. Here is an example from a Samhain meditation:

> *Tatters and homespun,*
> *dancing rags of black against firelight,*
> *arch of the heavens, starry arboretum,*
> *fairy light and backlit horizons.*
> *Walker, wagon dweller, black wolf,*
> *dark eyes of the night staring forthright, unblinking.*
> *Lateen sailed Moon-ship, an outsider peeking in, sees,*
> *the black legged spider becoming in dancing the dance,*
> *for the gods and the goddesses, looking at beauty,*
> *not to claim, absorb, or preserve it, but to live it,*
> *to be in life, the art of living with joy and frolic,*
> *love, harming none, wrapped in the cloak of the night,*
> *warding harm by the power of the stars and of life.*

The scenes and quotes in this next example came from a dream I prepared for with a meditative request for a totem animal. The whole vision was very lushly green, with the sense of place being one where the temperature is cool and it rains a lot—Ireland, England, or perhaps even the Pacific Northwest—and there was literally music in the air throughout, leaving me feeling very light-hearted and content. At the time of the dream, I had not even considered calling upon Epona, the Celtic goddess of the horse. The opening of the subconscious to other awareness sometimes brings delightful suprises.

Epona

The rain fell gently, mistily, and filled my heart
*   with song;*
I longed then for the elder wood and fair domains
*   long gone.*
"Epona!" cried I, "Epona! Send me the wild mares!"
I sought white steeds all sleek with rain to take me from
*   my cares.*

The wind uprose; across the tor the hoofbeats
*   sounded sharp;*
The air was split with wild shrieks as horses cleared
*   the mark.*
The great white beasts with tangled manes then
*   galloped into view;*
They tossed their heads and stamped their feet, and that
*   was when I knew—*

The wild mares were what I loved—the race against
*   the wind;*
I leaped upon the second steed and rode off with a grin.
"Epona!" I laughed, "Epona! You heard my call to thee!
You sent me wild mares to ride across the elder sea!"

You may want to keep a journal for your meditations and your creative communications. Review the journal entries once in awhile to see your development and check on your spiritual progress.

Find a tree that seems to reach out to you—it could be in your own yard (which is really best as it is close to you and your home), or you could encounter it while walking in a park or the woods.

— Meditation —
Tree Blending

For a planned meditation, take a ritual bath first. Place in a muslin pouch some herbs such as rosemary, sage, thyme, and marjoram, to attune your body and the tree to your earth connection. Scented soaps should not be too perfumy, but more *green*—floral smells are not recommended, instead use a *viney* scent such as black currant, or a *shrubby* scent such as mulberry. The reason for this is that vines, shrubs, and bushy or weedy herbs are simply more akin to trees in their understatement than flowers, which tend to be more showy. After your bath, dress in something comfortable and loose.

For this meditation, you may want a soft blanket to sit on. Find a tree that seems to reach out to you—it could be in your own yard (which is really best as it is close to you and your home), or you could encounter it while walking in a park or the woods. Walk around the tree and see which part seems to be the face or front of the tree. Although trees usually have growth all around, and an all-encompassing awareness of their surroundings, they do have a face side. Find this side and spread your blanket in front of the tree so that you can sit on the blanket and face the tree. With additional familiarity, you may feel quite comfortable with your back leaning against the trunk of the tree, rather like a child reclining against a parent, but for this meditation, you will want to face the tree. Take a picnic lunch with something for you to eat and drink, and in a pail have a libation of water and perhaps plant food.

Sit on your blanket with your back straight, perhaps in a semi-yogic or cross-legged position. With the latter pose, if your legs ache after awhile, you can always simply draw them up for a time and sit with your arms wrapped around your knees.

Look at the tree and note its general shape and foliage, the spreading of its limbs, and the atmosphere surrounding it. Compare it against the background and look for the tree's aura, the glowing light that envelopes the tree. What color is it? Does the aura look like the tree is content or is there something bothering the tree? A white to pale blue aura indicates a loving, peaceful, and sympathetic tree. Yellow shows energy, but if tinged with brown, this could indicate that it does not feel well. Red shows an active tree that is interested in what happens in its surroundings, and possibly alert to dangers. A green tinge shows fertility and connection with the wilderness spirit.

A purple aura shows spiritual connection, but if the aura is violet the tree could feel hostility and need soothing before continuing with the meditation. You can do this by placing a libation at the tree's roots. Watering the tree, nurturing it, adding fertilizer when it seems to need it, or planting a companion for the tree are all ways of soothing and establishing your acquaintance with a tree. Leaving a token of your esteem, such as decorations or delicate wind chimes, are ways of reaching out to the spirit of the tree to let it know that it is appreciated and loved by you.

As you sit before the tree, see the way it sets into the ground. Are the roots spread out? Does the trunk seem to simply dive into the earth? Visually examine the texture and grain of the bark.

Remain on the blanket, but now feel yourself move closer to the tree. See the tree observing you as you have observed the tree. Look for a crevice in the bark, and visualize yourself sliding into that crevice. Feel the woody texture of the trunk, strong and able to support the weight of the branches and foliage heavy upon the core that is the tree's body—your body.

As the tree, fluids course up and down your interior. You feel the gentle motion of tiny insects making their home about in the bark—your outer skin. Move your attention upward and feel yourself extending into the branches. You are moving in a multitude of directions, spreading upward to form a single entity with consciousness in your branchings, a myriad of thin twiggings and stemmings, attached to the stiffly subtle, opened leaves. Buddings are encased, about to open with the sunlight, but other leaves are spread, and you are aware of the sunlight activating the cells of your greenness.

Now you begin to understand that the essence of the tree has a face to the front of the trunk, but a consciousness that reaches to all levels so that as you channel upward through the branches to the topmost leaves, you are still aware and connected to the earth. The air is breezy at the top, and the sun is full upon you. Perhaps you find the height dizzying at first, but the tree laughs and you relax. You will not fall from this place, for you are part of it. The leaves and thin branches sway in the slight wind, and you feel yourself looking down.

There, far below, is someone sitting on a blanket, trance-like, gazing at the tree. Ah, that is you. The tree senses the not-tree within and gently directs you back through the twigs and down to the wider branches. You pause to feel the roughness of a bird's nest, and smile with admiration at the construction. Now you turn around the main trunk and feel the narrow gap in the trunk, a rounded opening into the trunk with a woody interior. You wrap yourself into that interior and feel the sensation of comfort, security, and home. It is a nest for another bird family. Now you are aware that your limbs are being groomed, tiny beaks poke into your bark and snatch away insects roaming along your skin. You continue downward, through the heartwood of the tree.

You are back at the main trunk, standing upright there, seeing you seeing yourself back. You smile and feel the tree relax in a sensation of camaraderie. It wants to show you something. Now you feel your toes—your roots—and the featherings of your roots deep in the earth. You let yourself travel downward still, past the level of the ground, and into the soil. Your texture changes here, and you realize with a warm glow that you are being entrusted with a journey into the most delicate part of the tree—its defenseless roots that surround the heart of the living tree.

"Harm the root, and you kill me," the tree tells you. "Cut the bark all around and the food of the soil cannot reach the rest of me and this too will kill me."

You tremble with the knowledge that this tree has shared with you.

"I am mighty and strong, but there is always danger in life, even one that lasts as long as centuries."

"All life comes to an end," you send your thought to the tree.

The tree smiles and indicates again the roots. You feel the smooth moist roots with their bristly fibers and hairlings drawing water and nourishment from the surrounding soil, and then you see them. The children of the tree. Little fingerlings and seedlings, pods waiting to open, and you know before the tree confides to you.

"There is no ending to life, only transformation."

And you know this is true, for never did a tree not speak true.

Listen to what else the tree has to say to you.

You take one more look at the soil deep beneath the surface of the earth, feel how your tree-feet are spread, wrapped around rocks, with little creatures sliding around the featherings of your roots. You move back up the woody trail back to the surface of the earth where grasses play in the breeze at your earth-level roots and a bee buzzes past you looking for a flower.

Seeing yourself again, you slide from out between the rough edges of the bark and back into your body.

You take a deep breath, hold it a moment, then exhale. Another deep breath, exhale, and you return to full awareness. Stand up and take the pail of water (perhaps mixed with plant food) and gently splash it around the roots of the tree. Touch your heart with your hand, then the tree trunk, your third eye region, and again the tree trunk. This is the blessing given and received—now you may sit again and eat your picnic meal and drink a cool beverage.

10

What About Familiars
and the Tarot?

Familiars

One of the traditional images of witchcraft is the ever-present familiar. The term "familiar" actually came from the fascination of early Christianity with good and evil dichotomies. A familiar is what a domestic servant in the home of a Roman Catholic bishop is called, so when the persecution of witches took off in earnest, the witch was expected to have servants that were the counterpart of those of the bishop. Hence, the idea of witches having demonic servants called familiars came to be documented by those who were persecuting the people who held to the Old Religion.

The basis for the spirit or demonic servant can be drawn from the old associations of certain animals with particular pagan deities. Hera had her peacock with the thousand eyes, Athena had her owl, Hecate had her raven, Diana had her deer, the Lady and the Lord of the Wildwood had their deer and stag, Cernunnos (and Shiva) had their snakes, Hel had her hounds, and so forth. Typical familiars for the Christian era naturally enough were snakes, dogs, owls, and ravens. In a short time, toads, frogs, and lizards joined the list as creative imaginations worked at identifying certain creatures as loathsome, and then associating these animals with practicing pagans. Left to the new deities were fish, doves, sheep, and lambs. Bulls and horses, which played important roles in pagan religions, were simply too valuable to defile. Perhaps that is why cats became a handy substitute. No one truly understood the valuable service provided by cats in keeping down the rat population until the felines were nearly wiped out and the plague hit Europe. Besides, cats were highly respected in the religious traditions of ancient Egypt, and Egypt was regarded as home to mysterious magics and sorceries.

So what about today's association of the witch and his or her familiar? Many people like to consider their pets as their friends or their familiars, which is another, legitimate, definition of the term. There are indeed Craft, or spirit, familiars, but not all cats, dogs, toads, and snakes are familiars simply because their human companion is a witch. You can tell a familiar from a pet by the eyes. A familiar has a certain intelligence in the eyes that goes beyond the expression normally found in similar animals. A familiar is indeed a spirit or energy that inhabits a form. The form may be a willing host to such an energy, in which case the entity may not always be present. In this sense, the animal becomes the channel through which the energy flows when the witch needs that contact.

A familiar may also be totally incorporated into the form. In this case, the entity created its physical form. This type of familiar is one that you will most likely see in a vision or dream before you encounter the living creature. There is purpose in this visitation. Usually, a familiar turns up after a witch has thought on the desirability of companionship in her or his magical practice.

Another way to determine if your pet is actually a familiar is by the animal's interest in your work, being around your Craft items, and appropriately participating in your magics. If the animal merely knocks things over and trips you in the circle, it is most likely a pet, but not a familiar. However, if the animal delicately touches your spell materials at the right time, sits quietly in the circle and watches the activity, or in some other way demonstrates a willingness to help and lend supportive energy, you may well have a familiar.

Should your pet be a familiar, you may want to perform a dedication ritual. The spirit entity will bond closer to you and be a greater helper after such a ceremony, and you will find communication easier and more productive. A sample ritual appears at the end of this chapter.

Historical Tarot

The very act of divination in witchcraft requires a link with the Lunar aspect of the Divine, Hecate, Bendidia, Artemis, and Isis, who are traditionally recognized today as goddesses of witches. The typical traditional methods of divination included scrying by smoke, crystal ball, palmistry, and tea leaves, along with dream interpretation. By the fifteenth century, tarot cards gained a following in Europe.

While there are a variety of opinions about how the tarot came to Europe, one of the plausible views is that the Romany Gypsies, migrating from India through Eastern Europe and into Northern Italy, brought the cards with them. Over the centuries, the cards were alternately embraced by secular rulers, as the card game of *tarocchi*, and banned by Christian church leaders. The tarot nevertheless survived repeated attempts by the clergy to eliminate them. These cards of East Indian origin remained in Europe and were soon adapted to provide the user with a Judeo-Christian interpretation of divination. While there are now a variety of versions of the tarot, and some dispute over how it became a tool of divination rather than being simply a game, the cards have been and continue to be a popular method of divination. Differences of opinion on the exact lineage of the tarot continue, with about the only consensus being that the tarot is not of European origin.

The cards of the major arcana encompass the archetypes of various powers, cosmic fates, and universal imagery. By comparing an original tarot deck of 1450 Milan, made at a time when the Romany Gypsies were moving into northern Italy, and the generally typical modern version of the tarot, the reworking of the original pagan concepts may be traced. Playing cards were first seen in India, with the symbols relating to the acoutrements of the Great Goddess Durga. Although playing cards have been mentioned in historical records in the century before the Sforza deck, those cards did not have the major arcana, which appears with the Sforza tarot. This could have been because the original major arcana was quite foreign to Europeans and it took a little time to adjust the characterizations to recognizable Western Pagan tradition.

It was in Renaissance Italy that the major arcana came into the tarot deck, and the Visconti Sforza Tarocchi Deck (named for the Duke of Milan, 1450 C.E.) of handpainted cards is the most complete surviving deck from that time period. The cards may be seen today, but to view them all you will have to visit three different museums and archives in Italy, since the deck was divided up for display. Four of the original cards are missing—the Devil, Tower, 3 of Swords, and Knight of Coins—and these have been recreated using Medieval and Renaissance themes, for a modern facsimile deck.

The Sforza deck is unusual for the heavy influence of European paganism on the cards. The cards of this earliest-known tarot deck do not have names or numbers written on the major arcana, thus the interpretation is more intuitive. Since cards originally represented an Indian paganism with reverence for the dark aspect of the divine, as seen in such deities as Durga, Kali, and Shiva, the tarot could be adapted to European pagan symbolism, but I feel it is not well-suited to the later incorporation of Judeo-Christian interpretation and dichotomy.

I prefer to see the tarot with pagan interpretations that reflect Green Witchcraft. The use of the devil imagery, kabbalistic references, the negative association with the Moon, and the misrepresentation of the Fool are a few examples of how the original feel of the tarot has been altered. Several newer decks have attempted to return to a more pagan perspective, notably the Old Path, Witches, Herbal, Norse, Celtic, Londa, and Dragon Tarots, but even these have retained some ties to the redrawn decks of later centuries, rather than to the original connection of the fifteenth century. A lovely Renaissance Tarot is also available for readings, with illustrations adapted from a number of fifteenth through eighteenth-century European paintings. It is perhaps the closest to the original in spirit.

There has been an attempt in recent years to deflect the negativity of the Devil card into a positive image of Pan or the Horned God. This can be a card of natural blessing, of matters taking their natural course, or attunement with nature, yet many decks still present this card as temptations and a bondage to material things. The Tower card is another card whose meaning is often interpreted as negative, but I prefer to see it as one of sudden understanding that results in rapid freedom from old ideas and constrictions. You know that major things are happening very fast when you draw both the Death card and the Tower card.

Card Reading

When doing a reading, whether with tarot cards or playing cards, the meaning of the card must be read in relation to the information sought, question asked, or the surrounding cards. So when you see a list of meanings for a card, not all of these apply in any given throw. Instead, the list is intended as a guideline for what some of the possible interpretations might be, but the real meaning comes from the psychic understanding of the reader. If you see a vision or sense a strong meaning in a card which is not listed, then that is the meaning being conveyed to you.

The tarot is a tool of mediumship, or channeling, that brings the reader into contact with a small portion of the energies of the universe to address a particular question or problem, or to simply offer guidance and comfort. Do not be afraid of using the gifts given to you if your interpretation does not fit that of a card's description.

Individual tarot decks have a unique feel to them as well. You may want to acquire several different styles of tarot decks to use in accordance with the occasion or type of reading involved. I find that I change general tarot decks with the seasons, but I will also be drawn to decks depending on the reading. As a result, I have accumulated quite a collection of tarot cards.

With regular playing cards, you may find that one particular deck *works* for you while others do not. You might want to set that deck aside and reserve it strictly for readings. I have used such a deck for card games such as solitaire and also for companion games such as gin rummy, and the only problem with doing so was that meanings and associations kept popping up. So now I prefer to keep my divination cards separate from playing cards.

The following interpretations are made within a pagan context, but you may alter them according to the imagery of your own tarot decks. The meanings are much the same in playing cards, with only the archetype cards and the Page cards missing. This is not really a great loss, since the primary meaning of the Pages is "news coming." The suit determines the type of news, and that may also be found in the eights. The archetype cards demonstrate a heavy emphasis on a particular meaning, all of which are also found in the other playing cards.

Reverse and Multiples Meanings

With reverse meanings, there are times when I feel there is no purpose for them to be read in the major arcana, and other times when I sense that they should be retained and used in a throw. The major arcana in particular has been interpreted by other readers as having only the upright position. The very *power* of the card makes it unnecessary to read a reverse position, so that every time a major arcana card appears reversed, the reader simply moves it into an upright position prior to reading the spread. You should follow your intuition for this. I think there is no such thing as a reversed ace. Aces are the power cards of the minor arcana, and they represent a generous flow of energy. While some readers will attribute a reverse interpretation for aces, I never do, and thus there are none listed here.

The multiple appearance in a spread of a particular number shows a greater influence of that type of card. Thus, throwing two, three, or four 10s provides the reader with additional information. If there are two or more types of multiples, try to put their meanings together for a coherent reading: four 10s and two Queens, for example, could be interpreted as a celebration involving a group of women. If there are cards of pregnancy, perhaps it is a baby shower. If there are political or business cards, perhaps it is a celebration of success with women in authority. The other cards of the spread will help to show the way to the appropriate interpretation where multiples are concerned.

Major Arcana Tarot Meanings

Aspects of the Craft relate to various cards, and these are noted after the interpretations. The Sabbats, Esbats, and Fairy Lore are all represented in the tarot, along with practitioners of the Craft and different sides of the goddess and the god. The primary names are more usually seen in tarot decks, but for some cards the names in parentheses are added to aid in pagan focusing. The numerical value for these cards varies between decks with the cards for Strength, Justice, Chariot, and Wheel of Fortune. Note: (R) stands for reversed.

0 — The Fool (Green Man)

Awakening; fearless courageousness; hidden potential—like the kernel in a seed—about to be awakened; playing life by joyous imagination; creativity and fertility; start of a quest; an open mind; innocence and enthusiasm. Relates the God to Ostara by his awakening of Mother Earth at Spring.

(R) The seed is planted, now comes tending and then harvest; quest achieved; time to decide on a new objective; letting the work begun progress and develop in its own time, with nurturing and care to help it along the way to harvest.

1 — The Magician (The Witch)

Controlling one's own destiny; communication skills; power to effect changes; practical use of knowledge. Relates to a practice of the Craft through herbs, intuition, raised and directed power, and the Elementals.

(R) Hesitation to use one's knowledge; lack of self-confidence; impeded communications; unwillingness to create change.

2 — The High Priestess

Formulating a personal path to find and use hidden knowledge and insights; learning the meanings of mysteries; trusting in one's own innate wisdom. Relates to Imbolc and purification.

(R) Knowledge and skill come with increased understanding; working to trust innate wisdom; moving closer to hidden insights.

3 — The Empress (Mother Earth)

Renewal of the Earth; use of folk magics; fertility; abundance; fruit-fulness; pregnancy; nourishment; good health; bounty; domestic skills; inspiration; project completing. Relates to the Goddess at Ostara's Spring Equinox.

(R) Progress initially slow, but gains momentum with under-standing; greater potential exists than is initially recognized or used.

4 — The Emperor (Horned God)

Fertility; creating; initiation of plans; building project; accomplishments from one's leadership and personal power; satisfaction; protecting what is under one's control; husbandry. Relates to Litha's Summer Solstice.

(R) Able to bring ideas to life; rational approach to creative endeavors; authority; administrative and bureaucratic aspects of growth.

5 — The Hierophant (The High Priest)

Teaching of Green Wisdom and Magics through the use of ritual; honoring of the Divine through ceremonies; incorporation of the Divine into all aspects of daily life; celebration rites and seasonal observances; codifying and organizing spiritual insights; imparting knowledge to others; ritual used to guide intuitive power and magic.

(R) Mistaking the learning format for the spiritual truths; form treated as more important than spiritual or intuitive knowledge;

magics of formulae; power through manipulation of spiritual truths and energy; restrictions imposed by others or by society; connection with Divine energy is blocked by someone who filters small amounts to the Seeker; accepting a less personal connection to the Divine.

6 — The Lovers (Lord and Lady of Greenwood)

Insight from a unity of two separate parts linked as one; trust; partnership; freedom and joy in accepting what the heart feels; loyalty; commitment; acceptance of emotional ties; unity of heart and mind; new opportunities. Relates to the partnership, growth, and renewal of Beltane.

(R) Compromise may be necessary for a successful relationship or partnership, but without self-deprecation; self-worth retains value in union with others; inability to see how one's actions affect others; promise of growth through partnership not developing as quickly as desired.

7 — The Chariot (The Wagon)

Balance achieved through control and dominance; conquest; personal achievement; consolidation of power; successful action; self-confidence; good health; beginning new projects; gains from own efforts; worldly success; travel for business gains/related success; possible change of location for continued success; military service or work-related domestic move.

(R) Pause to consolidate gains; inaction; stagnation; stuck in old patterns; after achieving success, unwillingness to venture into new areas; depending on other cards and aspects around this one, there may be a development of health problems relating to muscles, joints, and bone structure.

8 — Strength (The Crone)

Ability to overcome obstacles or difficulties; unity of action and wisdom; power to purify or destroy; power wisely utilized; willpower; facing adversity fearlessly with self-confidence; passing through a difficult time into a rebirth.

(R) Power hidden to protect others; strength in reserve; reconciliation but with full awareness of need for compromise; overcoming difficulties through discretion; ability to see behind the motives of others.

9 — The Hermit (Father Time)

Movement from darkness into light; accumulated learning becomes enlightened knowledge; being a guide to others by example and instruction; teaching; new wisdom born from combination of experience and learning; life's accomplishments lead to a secure old age; wisdom comes in due course; all things in the fullness of time; events develop in their own time and cannot be rushed; all the pieces start to fall into place. Relates to the ending and beginning of the Solar Year at Yule's Winter Solstice.

(R) Learning through personal experience begins; warning against being misled by the seeming wisdom of others; times are about to change; old ways give way to the new; progress; growth; be prepared to adapt to newer concepts; take care in choosing one's guide in all areas of learning; youthful outlook aids in the process of educational growth.

10 — The Wheel of Fortune (The Wheel)

Fortunes improve; changes for the better; youthful folly develops into mature wisdom; progress; fate; destiny; not all improvements come from one's own effort; stroke of good luck.

(R) New goals replace old ones; evolution and devolution; transition; Universe in motion; not all changes are for the better, but even these are transitory; things will improve; there is hope for the future. Relates to the concept of Fate as part of Chaos in that there are times when the load is carried by competent, knowledgeable people, but the benefits are felt by those who do little to earn them.

11 — Justice (The Scales)

Law of Equal Returns; fairness; truth guides the balance in legal matters; Justice through an agent on one's behalf; equity.

(R) Implicit in the law of *what is sent comes back* is the balance of *what has been sent may be returned*; retribution wields the sword of Justice on behalf of the aggrieved; rewards appropriate to actions; warning against idleness, which has no reward; call upon the Divine to balance the scales.

12 — The Hanged Man (The Shaman)

Vision quest; meditation; inaction while weighing the choices; suspended activity; letting matters take their own course without interference; revelation sought and received; some self-sacrifice for gains; give to receive; seeking answers from the subconscious.

(R) Action decided upon; revelations from meditation put into use; pushed into making a decision by external forces.

13 — Death (The Lord of Shadows)

Insight leads to transition and transformation; change; end of one project and the start of a new one; cutting down old ideas/works to let new ones sprout; a turning point in life; optimism for the future; awareness prepares one to remove old opposition. Relates to the mystical Samhain closeness of the Shadowland and Otherworld.

(R) Making changes and teaching others; prompting change in others; self-evaluation; resisting change.

14 — Temperance (Balance)

Harmony between the rational and the intuitive minds; interaction between ideals and reality invigorating both; balance between physical and psychic realms; agreement between opponents; truce; overcome present difficulties; patience; reconciliation; trusting one's own intuition; skill in the arts; new life breathed into one's health, work, goals. Relates to the veneration of natural springs and seeking healing and peace at these sites.

(R) Disharmony; holding onto one's own ideas; attitude of no compromise; confined to old notions; over-emphasis on either physical or psychic leads to imbalance; stagnant approach to challenges; revitalization coming; a return to one's source of inspiration.

15 — The Devil (Destroyer)

If you or your tarot deck uses Pan or The Horned God, the (R) is the upright reading, and the upright reading is the (R).

Willing bondage to a way of life or attitudes that one does not enjoy or like; potential held in check; energy held impotent; fear of change; self-imposed sterility in areas of life and spirit; uncertainty over which path to choose; unnecessary worries over unimportant matters tie one to fears; bondage to form over substance; self-destructive behavior; self-inflicted unhappiness.

(R) Unleashing potential; setting oneself free from self-imposed restrictions or unhappiness; release of inhibitions; making a decision for change for the better; regaining control of one's destiny; liberation.

16 — The Tower (The Wild Hunt)

Sudden change; old beliefs toppled by enlightenment; world turned upside down as one's Universe changes; destruction of falsity through revelation; secrets revealed; truth that was deliberately hidden is set free; the Eclipsed Sun bursts forth with its corona and releases the Star of Enlightenment; inner spirit erupts from the confinement of dogma. Relates to the freeing of the spirit by the Rade of the Wild Hunt.

(R) Self-revelation leads to changes; movement from indecision to action; confusion is past and one can now think clearly; new healing begun.

17 — The Star

Hope; creativity; inspiration; opportunity; ability to reach for the Star of Enlightenment while keeping one's feet on the ground; drawing manifested benefits from contact with one's Sidhe-Self; ability and talent is recognized by others. Relates to Fairy blessings or wishes granted.

(R) Seeking creativity and success; need for peace and release of past tensions; use subconscious for problems/answering questions.

18 — The Moon

Walking between the worlds, yet being part of both; waters of creation; learning the magics of the Moon Goddess; putting aside preconceived ideas to contemplate a matter anew; discovery of the hidden; exposing deception; introspection; leap of subconscious to fully comprehend reality; finding inner truths from the subconscious mind; reflective thoughts; trusting one's intuition; renewal; psychic dreams and awareness. Relates to the Lunar Esbats.

(R) Disconnection with the duality of existence; self-denial; limiting the imagination; unawareness of facades; warning of deception; decision between being true to oneself or to duty.

19 — The Sun

Success; contentment; mental and spiritual growth; material happiness; satisfying achievements; joy of life without fear, guilt, or hatred; revitalization. Relates to the height of power of the Oak King and the energy of Lughnassadh that produces a bountiful harvest.

(R) Burdens will soon be lifted; temporary delay to success; answer to problems will soon be discovered; efforts will be rewarded.

20 — Judgement (Harvest)

Good choices have been made; potential fulfilled; time to be honest with oneself; awakening; change for the better; renewed energy; restored health; atonement; rebirth. Relates to the Mabon harvest of the wine of life.

(R) Gaining knowledge from the past; learning from past mistakes; by taking stock of one's past with the desire for improvement, one may be reborn into a new life.

21 — The World (The Universe)

Wholeness and totality; Union with the All; the Cosmic Dancer leads one in joyful dance through the cycles of the Universe; success; perfection; achievement; joy; attainment of one's objectives; completion; end of an era; a matter is concluded.

(R) Striving for greatness; seeking attainment; rebirth into a new life about to begin; transition; materialism becomes insignificant compared to the Infinite.

Summary of the Archetypes

Major Arcana

Fool: Enthusiasm; open-minded; start/end quest; originality; holiday
  (R) Quest achieved; rest; plan new goals.
Mage: Control own destiny; initiative; wider audience; diplomacy.
  (R) Overly intellectual; hesitant to use own power.
Priestess: Intuition; insight; mysteries understood; wisdom;
  between worlds.
  (R) Comprehension less than desired; insight clouded.
Empress: Inspiration; abundance; ability; intellect; creativity; dialogue.
  (R) Progress is slow at first.
Emperor: Reason dominates; power; builder; responsibility;
  authority; will.
  (R) Energized activity; ideas come to life.
Priest: Scholarly; intellectual; spiritual energy; organized; teach(er/ing).
  (R) Divine inspiration; overly traditional.
Lovers: Partnership; trust; choice; examination; ties; attempt.
  (R) Appreciation of self-worth; reaching to others; obsessive.
Chariot: Merit recognized; balance by will/control; success;
  goal-focused.
  (R): Direction found; action now; release of aims.
Strength: Willpower; courage; obstacles overcome; control/
  direct power.
  (R) Power used with kindness; emotionalism.
Hermit: Search for enlightenment; things in due time;
  wisdom; prudence.
  (R) Withdraw to reflect; learning begins.
Wheel: Destiny; changes in life; fortune improves;
  progress; opportunity.
  (R) Moving to next goal in life; small gains.
Justice: Fairness; virtue; equilibrium; harmony; natural law; agent
  at work.
  (R) Appropriate rewards; imbalance.
Hanged Man: Inner peace; activity suspended; meditation;
  delay; idealism.
  (R) Knowledge put to use; decision made; time for action; sacrifice.

Death: Rapid change; endings/beginnings; turning point; negative cleared.

(R) Self-evaluation; teaching others; impediment.

Temperance: Moderation; balance; trust intuition; patience; unity; reflect.

(R) Emotional; intuitive; too compliant.

Horned God: Natural course; harmony with Nature; magnetism; naturalism.

(R) Self-bondage; agitation; form greater than substance.

Tower: Sudden change from enlightenment; self-revelation.

(R) Need strong foundation.

Star: Inspiration; opportunity; hopes attainable; peace.

(R) Seeking success and creativity; sense of insecurity.

Moon: Intuitive; visions; trips; fulfillment; seeing beneath the surface.

(R) Facades; delusions and illusions.

Sun: Harmony; joy; achievement; mental/spiritual growth; unity.

(R) Answers found; strain.

Judgement: Renewal; harvest; rebirth; atonement; health.

(R) Hesitancy; learning from past mistakes.

World: Reward; wholeness; success; promotion; achievement.

(R) Striving for greatness; burdens.

Minor Arcana

The areas addressed by each suit of the minor arcana are stated after the suit item. Other names for the suits are given in parentheses. When doing a reading, look to see which suit(s) predominate in the spread to understand the focus of the cards. Sometimes the cards want to address a subject other than the one questioned, so it may be helpful to read such a spread first, just to see what the Universe is trying to tell the questioner. Then try doing another spread for the originally asked question.

Cups: Emotions, Love, Heart, Friendship

Ace: Abundance; joy; positive change; inspiration; fount of life.

2: Intuition manifested; emotional balance; love; partnership; affinity.
(R) Misunderstanding; indulgence; unappreciation.

3: Good news received; vitality; happy conclusion; relief; luck.
(R) Over-indulgence.

4: Success; desire for new challenges; love; new
possibilities; friendship.
(R) Inaction; discontent; aversion.

5: Sharing abundance; festivities; inheritance; patrimony to protect.
(R) Difficulties overcome; some loss, but assets remain.

6: Renewal; shared energy; spiritual communication; harmony;
happy future.
(R) Living in the past; resisting change.

7: Success; gains in love; considering choices carefully; opportunity.
(R) Fear of failure; unable to decide; gifts rejected.

8: Reason; moderation; turning point in life; discarding old path
for new.
(R) Continued effort leads to joy; dissatisfaction brings changes.

9: Victory; prosperity; satisfaction; good intuition; happy future.
(R) Self-satisfaction; impressions not accurate.

10: Happiness; recognition; rest; enjoyment of family and friends.
(R): Passing friendships; quarrels; casual friendships.

Page: Emotions satisfied; practical use of talents; creative expression.
(R): Newness; love notes; indiscretion; unfulfillment.

Knight: opportunity; inspiration; close friend; relaxations.
(R): Ideas need work to succeed; opportunistic cooperation.

Queen: Romanticism; nurturing; creative; artistic; psychic/
emotional ties.
(R) Emotional changes; ambivalent feelings.

King: Counselor; creative need; intuition; business/law; ready
for talks.
(R) Obstacles; no movement; self-promoting; changeability.

Pentacles (Coins): Finances, Business

Ace: Big commercial success; happiness; earnings; growth; business sense.

2: Balance by effort/talent; energy for goals; relocation; skills learned.
(R) Difficulties; news; effort needed.

3: Celebrity; powerful support; rewards; skill in Craft/work; pregnancy.
(R) Indifference.

4: Small gift; endurance; gentle power; financial security.
(R) Delays; uncertainties; losses.

5: Rewards lie ahead; feeling entrenched; obstacles; financial worries.
(R) Relief comes; courage to find hidden opportunities.

6: Gifts; gratified; rewards; bonus; sincerity; generosity.
(R) Overspending; avarice; illness.

7: Goals achieved; productivity; recovery; business start; perseverance.
(R) Effort does not pay off as well as expected.

8: Increase through own effort; commercial ability; work rewarded; promotion.
(R) Lack of ambition or trust.

9: Accomplishment; prudence; growth; discernment; sudden luck; security.
(R) Growth halted; health cares.

10: Joy; earnings; stability; favorable placement; good investments; wealth.
(R) Changes; disruptions; money worries.

Page: Diligence; completion; news from child; new lifestyle/identity/work.
(R) Energy used; need more study.

Knight: Useful person; propitious occasion; goals gained; career; ability.
(R) Moving too quickly; recklessness.

Queen: Culture; stability; plans realized; practical ambitions; freedom.
(R) Delays; self-indulgent.

King: Economic power; ideas manifested; sensible/methodical speculations.
(R): Inability; traditionalist.

Swords: Strength, Power, Conflicts, Worries

Ace: Triumph; power to achieve goals; strength; breakthrough; success; strong mind; intellectual power; victory; conquest.

2: Harmony of action; balance of opposing forces; problem resolved.
(R) Tenuous peace; duplicity.

3: New path needs courage; conflict/talks resolves problem; absence.
(R) Fear of loss; need for understanding; confusion.

4: Peace; readiness gives security; rest; order; resolved conflict; alert.
(R) Meditation; discretion.

5: Force used for good; domination; stealth for goals; fear of defeat.
(R) Parting of ways.

6: Success from self-sacrifices; troubles left behind/controlled; trip.
(R): Displacement; troubled; hindrance due to selfishness.

7: Artistic energy; hope; confidence; diplomacy; creative action; reveries.
(R) Frustration; plans postponed; attempts made.

8: Patience; goals obstructed; actions need care; don't turn from path.
(R) New options; fears end; health improves.

9: Plans about to be realized after worries; need better communication.
(R) Deception; opposition raises doubts.

10: Turning away from present troubles; exhaustion; sadness.
(R) Things improve with courage and will power.

Page: Vigilance; matter resolved; careful preparation; language skills.
(R) Cunning; obstructions; hindered.

Knight: Career activity; ability; courage; good balance of power; smart.
(R) Headstrong; ideas yet unformed.

Queen: Taking action; determined; perceptive; independent/focused mind.
(R) Impractical; separation; sadness.

King: Decisions made/methods implemented; legal action; authority; will.
(R) Indecision; willfulness draws resistance to plans.

Wands (Rods): Career, Study, Creative Ventures

Ace: Creation; invention; beginning an enterprise; new ideas; discussions.

2: Fulfillment; strong personality; earned success; good advice; new goals.
(R) Gains less than desired; suffering.

3: Business gains; unity for success; negotiations; initiative; planning.
(R) Troubles end; learning facts

4: Serenity; romance; unexpected occasion; teamwork; spiritual camaraderie.
(R) Rewards are small.

5: Overcome obstacles; conflict brings change; renewal of efforts.
(R) Contradictions; complexities.

6: Triumph after difficulties; good news; self-expression; understanding.
(R) Disloyalty; insurmountable odds.

7: Success; obstacles overcome; trust intuition; enterprise completed.
(R) Doubts; handle problems one at a time to avoid energy drain.

8: Letter/news coming soon from a distance; travel; quick action.
(R) Self-analysis; creative tension; journey cancelled.

9: Deeper awareness; strength in adversity; readiness; help from others.
(R) Delays; obstacles; over-protectiveness.

10: Plans realized; determination; delegate duties; don't do others' work.
(R) Difficulties; plans set aside; oppression; over-committed.

Page: Completion; energy; new cooperations/ideas; message; reliable friend.
(R) Impatience; petty rivalries; uncertainties.

Knight: Enterprising; ambitious; energetic; journey; movement.
(R) Discord; plans change; departure.

Queen: Sincerity; practical; self-knowledge/mastery; friendly confidant.
(R) Search for durable relationships; desires.

King: Conscientious; direct action taken; follow council; good relations.
(R) Austerity; desire for action dulled by criticism.

Multiples of Cards

Ace: New Beginnings
4: fast action; start new life
3: swift gains; quick success
2: change afoot at work/home

Two: Balance; Conflicts
4: teamwork; reorganization/ shakeup
3: talks(gossip) w/fast conclusions;
   need to reorganize

Three: Career
4: well-rewarded; strong finish
3: very eventful time; lies nearby

Four: Attainment
4: foundation firm; need vacation
3: industrious; demanding work

Five: Fulfillment
4: doing well; sudden confrontation
3: sense of well-being

Six: Decisions
4: time to sort things out; peace
3: confusion; gather information

Seven: Changes
4: slow down; flow with changes
3: contracts; help from friends

Eight: Communications
4: quick news; evaluation needed
3: travel; commerce

Nine: New Path
4: responsibilities; old ways ending
3: active communications;
   correspondence

Ten: Success/Tallies
4: joy; celebration; family
3: much buying and selling

Page: News/Young People
4: creativity; ideas; school news
3: good news on the way
2: social gatherings; games
   of chance

Knight: Direction/Thoughts
4: swift action; crisis brewing
3: honors; rest period
2: old friends; reminiscences

Queen: Authority/Women
4: local government; words a
   powerful force
3: influence; discretion at present
2: groups of women

King: Power/Men
4: politics; VIP meetings

3: award, honor in sight
2: groups of men

Lady and Lord, I hold you in honor and know that I am one with all the things of the Earth and Sky. My kin are the trees and the herbs of the fields; the animals and stones of the seas and the hills. The fresh waters and deserts are built out of thee, and I am of you and you are of me.

— Ritual —
Dedicating a Familiar

Since this ritual involves an animal, you will be better off not using candles at the Quarters. You may want to use rocks, gems, or stones around your circle, or nothing at all. This can be done in conjunction with an Esbat, but I recommend doing this as its own ritual when the Moon waxes halfway to Full. This Half Moon can represent the bridge between dark- and light-sided magics. The animal should be one that has indicated through its behavior that it is receptive to this kind of connection. Baby animals should not be dedicated as familiars, but you can always present them to the Divine as creatures in your care. This could be done with an adaptation of the Wiccaning ritual from my earlier book, *Green Witchcraft*.

On your altar, light an incense with a pine or woodsy scent, or burn mugwort herb.

Have the following items on the altar: something to designate the god and the goddess sides of the altar, the incense and burner, matches, small bowl of water, small dish of salt (rock or sea salt), a pentacle, a small cauldron, a brown (or cinnamon) votive candle and container, candle snuffer, anointing oil, knife (athame), wand, a cup or goblet containing juice or wine, some cake or a muffin, and food and water for the animal (the example here will be for a cat).

Circle and Greetings

Gently sweep the circle deosil (N-E-S-W) with your besom, and say:

> *As I sweep this circle, may it be cleansed and made ready for my work.*

Stand before the altar, clap your hands three times, and say:

> *The circle is about to be cast and I freely stand within to greet my Lady and my Lord.*

With the knife lowered, walk around the circle and envision a blue light shooting from the tip to form the circle's boundary, and say:

This is the boundary of the circle, around me and through all barriers above and below, as a sphere is this circle in which only love shall enter and leave. I draw this circle in the presence of the Goddess of Earth and the God of the Wildwood, that it be a place where they may manifest and bless their child, _____ (Craft Name/Working Name), *and this creature of Nature.*

Put the knife on the altar and pick up the wand. Walk deosil (clockwise) around the circle, starting at the North and pausing at each Quarter (N-E-S-W) to call upon the Elemental, raising up your arms and wand, saying:

I call upon thee, Elemental Earth, to attend this rite and guard this circle, for we are kith and kin, thee and me.

I call upon thee, Elemental Air, to attend this rite and guard this circle, for we are kith and kin, thee and me.

I call upon thee, Elemental Fire, to attend this rite and guard this circle, for we are kith and kin, thee and me.

I call upon thee, Elemental Water, to attend this rite and guard this circle, for we are kith and kin, thee and me.

Return to the altar, set down the wand and put the tip of the knife into the dish of salt, saying:

Salt is purification, preservation, and life. I bless this salt to be used in the circle in the names of the Goddess and the God, _____ (Diana and Pan; Teiltui [Tell' sha] and Herne; or whatever names you choose to use).

Add three portions of salt to the water bowl, using the tip of the knife, and say:

Let the blessed salt purify this water for use in this circle. I consecrate and cleanse this water in the names of the Lady and the Lord, Teiltui, and Herne.

Take the consecrated water bowl and sprinkle water from it around the circle moving clockwise and say:

> *I consecrate this circle in the names of the Goddess of the Earth and the God of the Wildwood, Teiltui and Herne. This circle is conjured a Circle of Power that is purified and sealed.*

Return the bowl to the altar, take up the censor and move around the circle to cense it, then return it to the altar. Put a drop of anointing oil on your fingertip, make a Solar Cross on your forehead, then a Lunar Spiral over the Cross, and say:

> *I, _____, am consecrated in the names of the Lady and the Lord, Teiltui and Herne, in this their circle.*

Next are the Libations of Greeting. Set down the knife and pick up the cup of wine (or other beverage) and pour some into the cauldron to honor the Divine with the first draught, then take a sip from the cup.

Raise the wand in greeting, and say:

> *I, _____, who am your child, stand between the worlds and call upon my Lady of the Earth and my Lord of the Wildwood to hold communion with me. I affirm my joy of union with the Divine and acknowledge Your blessings upon me. What I send returns to me, and I conduct my Craft accordingly.*

Set the water bowl on the pentacle and hold the knife over it, and say:

> *Great Lady, bless this creature of Water and of Earth to Your service. May I always remember the cauldron waters of rebirth and the many forms of being. Of Water and Earth am I.*

Hold up the water bowl and say:

> *I honor You, Great Lady!*

Replace bowl on altar, put the censer on the pentacle, hold the knife over it, and say:

> *Great Lord, bless this creature of Fire and Air to Your service. May I always remember the sacred fire that dances within all life and hear the voices of the Divine. Of Fire and Air am I.*

Hold up the censer and say:

> *I honor You, Great Lord!*

Return the censer to the altar and hold up the goblet and say:

> *Power and Grace; Beauty and Strength are in the Lady and the Lord. Patience and Love; Wisdom and Knowledge; you are Endings, Passages, and Beginnings. I honor you both!*

Pour a second libation and take a second sip from the cup.

Dedication of the Familiar

With arms upraised, say:

> *Lady and Lord, Teiltui and Herne, I call out to Thee! I hold you in honor and know that I am one with all the things of the Earth and Sky. My kin are the trees and the herbs of the fields; the animals and stones of the seas and the hills. The fresh waters and deserts are built out of thee, and I am of you and you are of me.*

Lower your arms and gather your animal friend into your arms, and say:

> *I call upon you to grant my desire. Let me rejoice in my oneness with all things and let me love the life that emanates from my Lady and my Lord into all things. I know and accept the creed: that if I do not have that spark of love within me, I will never find it outside myself, for Love is the Law and Love is the Bond! And this do I honor when I give honor to the Lady and the Lord.*

Take a dot of anointing oil onto one finger and touch it to the brow of the cat, and say:

> *My Lady Teiltui and my Lord Herne, I bring before You Both this cat that she/he may be dedicated as my familiar to your honor. I will defend and protect thy spark within her/him as I would that within me, and I seek thy protection and defense of us both. You are our life and we are of You. So Mote It Be!*

Holding the cat gently, say:

> *Lady Teiltui and Lord Herne, you are the fullness of the earth and the protectors of the animals. I call upon you to receive the dedication of this cat as my companion in magic and friendship, that we may work together and with you. This cat, whom I have named _____ (pet's name), seeks a new name from you to serve as my familiar in the Craft. As my familiar will know me by the name you have given me, so do I now ask that you share with me the name you have given this cat, one that is secret between us. Tell me, my Lady and my Lord, what is my familiar's name.*

Listen quietly, petting and observing your cat, and hear the name from the Lady and the Lord. Do not be surprised if it is something quite odd. The names of familiars tend to be strange, and fairly descriptive of the animal by appearance or disposition. Names like Tom Tit, Hop and Spin, and Hearth Sitter are true witch names for familiars, so listen to what comes to you.

When you hear the name, then hold your cat to face you and say the name to your cat:

> *You are_____, and together, with the favor of the Lady and the Lord, through the blessings of the Elementals, do we share in the Craft.*

Waft some of the incense smoke to the cat. Dab a bit of the blessed water onto your finger and touch it to the cat and say:

Through Fire and Air, Water and Earth, are you made one with me in the working of my Craft, named by the Lady and Lord, and blessed by the Elementals.
So Mote It Be!

Set the cat down and say:

Great Lady and Great Lord, let my familiar be imbued through your power to aid me in my Craft.

Light the votive candle from the center candle, and say:

Let this small light illuminate the wilderness path to bring harmony and peace, health and companionship, between _____ (familiar's name) ***and me with the love and blessing of Nature.***

Cakes and Wine

The ritual ends with Cakes and Wine. With arms upraised, say:

I know of my needs and offer my appreciation to that which sustains me. May I ever remember the blessings of my Lady and my Lord.

Lower your arms, take up the goblet in the left hand and the knife in the right, and slowly lower the point of the knife into the wine, saying:

In like fashion does male join female for the happiness of both and the bounty of the Earth. Let the fruits of their union promote life and let the wealth of the earth spread throughout the lands.

Remove the knife, touch it to the cat's water bowl, then set the knife on the altar. Take a drink from the cup and return it back to the altar. Touch the knife to the cake (or bread) and then the cat's food, and say:

This food is the blessing of the Lady and the Lord to the living body. We partake of it freely and in communion with the source of life and one another.

Take a piece of the cake (bread) and drop it into the cauldron, saying:

> *All life feeds on life and returns to the cauldron for*
> *rebirth. I honor the passage of life through the Lady.*

Place the cat's food bowl and water bowl for her/him, and enjoy the companionship as you have your own meal. When finished, hold the knife over the altar and say:

> *Lord and Lady, I am blessed by your sharing this time*
> *with me; watching and guarding me, guiding me here*
> *and in all things. I came in love and I depart in love.*

Farewells and Opening the Circle

Raise the knife in a salute and say:

> *Love is the law and the bond. Merry did we meet,*
> *merry do we part, and merry will we meet again.*
> *Merry meet, merry part, and merry meet again!*
> *The circle is now cleared. So Mote It Be!*

Kiss the blade of the knife and set it on the altar.

Take up the wand and walk around the circle widdershins, pausing at each Quarter to raise your arms and wand and address the Elemental, saying:

> *Depart in peace, Elemental Earth! We have met in*
> *kinship thee and me. My blessings take with you!*

Lower arms, envision the Elemental leaving, move to the next Quarter until all four Elementals are farewelled.

Return to the altar and set down the wand. Raise your arms and say:

> *Beings and Powers of the visible and invisible, depart in*
> *peace! You aid in my work, whisper in my mind, bless*
> *me from realms of Shadow and Otherworld, and there*
> *is harmony between us. My blessings take with you.*
> *The circle is cleared.*

Take the knife and go to the North Quarter, proceed deosil around the circle envisioning the blue light being drawn back into the knife as you say:

The circle is open yet the circle remains as its magical power is drawn back into me.

Upon reaching the North again, touch the flat of the knife blade against your forehead and envision the blue light swirling around and back into you. Return to the altar, raise up the knife and say:

The ritual is ended. Blessings have been given and blessings have been received. May the peace of the Goddess and the God remain in my heart.
So Mote It Be!

Set the knife down and put away your tools. The libation cauldron is poured into a depression in the ground or washed down the drain as you envision it passing through channels and out to the sea.

Elemental Tarot Spread

This is a fast and easy spread that gives a quick answer to a simple question. Shuffle the cards as you concentrate on the question. Cut the deck into three stacks, then restack so the middle stack (the midhe of the tarot) is on top and the stack with the cards previously on top are now on the bottom. Lay out the first four cards face down in the form of the solar cross (equal-armed cross), saying:

One for the Earth,
One for the Air,
One for the Fire,
One for the Water.

Add the fifth card face down to the center of the cross, and say:

And one for the question.

Now lay out the next four cards face up in the cross, saying:

> *By Elemental Earth,*
> *By Elemental Air,*
> *By Elemental Fire,*
> *By Elemental Water.*

Add the fifth card face up to the center of the cross, and say:

> *Is the answer revealed.*

To read the spread, the last card is the answer to the question. If you are in a hurry and do not have the time to explore why it is the answer, that card will suffice. If you have a moment to check out the reason for that card, the face-up cards show the obvious factors surrounding the answer. Now turn up the face-down cards and see what the hidden factors are that affect the answer. In the center portion of the cross, the hidden card reflects what lies behind the answer to your question.

Appendix A

A Few Terms

Athame (a'tha-may or a-thaw'may): Ritual knife of witchcraft used to direct energy in magical work; generally a black-handled knife, but any knife or knife-like object used to conduct energy for magic work may be an athame.

Black Mirror: Tool used for divination and dark aspect meditations.

Bolline (bo-leen'): Practical knife of witchcraft used to cut with and inscribe objects; generally a white- or brown-handled knife, but some witches may use only one knife for the work of both the athame and bolline.

Casting Cloth: Layout cloth with appropriate markings, used for tossing the ogham fews (or for runes).

Charms: Objects made and infused with magical energy, and carried or placed to achieve a goal.

Circle of Power: Ritual area created to contain raised energy that may be directed in spellwork.

Curses: Contain malevolence to the sphere of the generator of the negative energy.

Dark Moon: Representative of the Goddess as the One Who Transforms in her aspect of Tomb and Womb.

Dark Power: Generally negative energies drawn from the Dark Aspects of the Goddess and the God.

Deflection: Defuse general malevolence and ill will of others.

Dressing: Putting an oil on spell items such as candles as part of a ritual consecration to prepare the object to attract and direct the energy of a spell to accomplish a goal.

Esbat (Es'bat): Lunar celebrations of witches during the Full and New Moons; often used in conjunction with spellwork.

Exorcism: Aid spirits in passage; disperse negative energies to allow positive energies to enter.

Familiar: Witch's animal or spirit helper in magical work.

Hallows: Sacred, holy, consecrated; a time when the veil between the worlds is thin and there is easy passage, hence the holy time of Hallow'een (Samhain).

Ken (Kenning): All-encompassing sensation of "knowing" something with a certitude and acceptance that what is kenned, is; keen, instinctive insight.

Light Power: Generally positive energies drawn from the Light Aspects of the Goddess and the God.

Lunar Eclipse: Emblem of the Goddess in her dark aspect as Crone, Tomb/Womb, and Transformer.

Magic: Creating changes by the gathering, focusing, and directing of energy.

Mannuz (Mah-nú): the Self as part of the Universe and the Divine.

Meditation: Altered state of awareness in which the conscious mind is subdued to let the subconscious mind functions dominate; state of relaxation and accessibility.

New Moon: Lunar phase symbolizing the Goddess in her aspect of Crone; Dark Lady, and Wisdom.

A Few Terms

Ogham: Old Celtic alphabet symbols named for trees and used for magical symbolism.

Oracle: Ancient location where divinations took place and prophecies were uttered, generally by priestesses.

Purgings and Releasings: Lesser exorcisms that cleanse and turn away negativity or impediments, absorb negativity to be buried for grounding, and dissipate negative energies.

Rade: "Ride"—the wild ride of the Hunter gathering the souls of the dead; passing of the Wild Hunt or the Rade is demonstrated by stormy weather and fast-moving, roiling black clouds in the sky.

Retribution: Return negative energy to the sender and seal it there by the added energy of herbs.

Return-to-Sender: Send back intentionally harmful negativity to its source.

Rituals: Magical or devotional ceremonies in which energy is raised and the practitioner is united with the Divine in religious observances, meditative states, or for the conducting of magic as with spell work.

Runes: Old Teutonic and Norse alphabet symbols associated with magical meanings.

Sabbat (Sab'bat'): Four solar and four agricultural celebrations of witches: the spring and fall equinoxes and summer and winter solstices, the harvests of August, September, and October, and the lambing time of February. Some people reverse the Sabbats for the Southern Hemisphere to align with seasonal changes, others prefer to celebrate according to the traditional European dates. It is a matter of personal preference.

Solar Eclipse: Emblem of the God in his aspects of Dark Lord, Lord of Shadows, Death, Chaos, Resurrection, Hunter, and Leader of the Wild Hunt.

Spells: Magic gathered and directed in ritual to achieve a goal.

Appendix A

Tarot (Tair'roe): Deck of seventy-eight cards originally used in the fifteenth century, in a game called *Tarrochi*, and now used mainly in divination; the deck contains twenty-one archetype cards called the Major Arcana, and those typical of regular playing cards, called the Minor Arcana, with the addition of a page or princess card for each suit.

Turning of the Wheel: Passing of the seasons of the Sabbats.

Appendix B

Names of Gods and Goddesses

The following is a glossary of dark aspect deity names which may be useful for ritual focus and connection. This selection includes gods and goddesses from the pantheons of India, Greece, Rome, and the Celtic lands. Depending on the subject of your rite or spell, some of these names (and the images they inspire) can enhance the flow of energy for you.

I particularly enjoy the forgotten meanings of February and March, and the types of rituals once practiced in those months. Today there are many cultures where the dead are honored with feasts, picnics, decorations, and family gatherings at gravesites to keep alive the memory of the departed and to express veneration for one's ancestors. These ceremonies are deeply moving as people contemplate their personal heritage and their connection with the people of the past. For them, death and the dark aspect of the divine are part of life, and that understanding adds to the quality of their lives.

Look over the listing, and if a particular deity represents an aspect you seek to work with, meditate on the deity name. When you sit in your meditation circle, light a black or deep purple candle and an incense like myrrh, frankincense, patchouli, or other scent that makes you think of the night and the deep earth. You may want to pat your seed gourd against your hand as you chant the name of the deity. Let the images come to you that are invoked by the sound of the name. If these images match or seem to work with what you are trying to accomplish, then by all means, use them. One obvious example of this would be to see if using the name of the goddess Angerona would be helpful in the black mirror meditation for name-knowing.

Gods

Arawn: Celtic god of the Underworld (called Annwyn).

Belatucados: Celtic horned god of war.

Cernunnos (Ker-nu'-nos): Stag-antlered god of Otherworld, death, resurrection, and the Wild Hunt; lord of animals and protector of wildlife.

Dionysus (Die'-oh-nee'-shahs): Ancient god of mysteries of death and rebirth symbolized by wine and cycles of vegetation; special followers were the maenads (women who became raging drunk), bac-chantes (more noisy revelers similar to the images of the Wild Hunt and followers of Shiva), and satyrs, all of whom set free the wild animal side of humanity and connected with the dark energy of Chaos.

Dis: Roman god of the Underworld, another name for Pluto and Hades in the aspect of keeper of riches.

Februus (Feb'bru-us): Etruscan dark lord of the Underworld, honored in the month name, February, during which time tombs were decorated and offerings of food and flowers were made to the dead.

Gwydion: God of magic.

Hades (Hay'-dees): Name of the shadowy god of the Underworld and the riches of the earth; his name has become synonymous with the Underworld.

Herne: British version of Cernunnos; lord of the wildwood.

Hiesi: Finnish god of sorcery and communication with the dead.

Kuvera: Earth god of India similar to Pluto/Hades in the association with the gem and mineral wealth of the earth and sexuality.

Lugh: Celtic sun god.

Mars: God of war, honored by the month of March; a deity of spring as well as battle skills.

Midhir: Underworld god whose domain was guarded by cranes.

Moros: Dark god of unknown destiny.

Morpheus: Dark god of deep sleep, psychic dreams, and death.

Pan: Earth god of rustic lifestyle and flocks; god of domestic animals; god of fertility; dark god of unreasoning terror and unknown fears.

Pluto: Another name for Hades, god of the Underworld.

Pwyll: Underworld god.

Shiva (Shee'-va): Pre-Hindu god of India encompassing many attributes including lord of animals and king of the dance, in the latter aspect, he dances creation to its destruction to become part of the All and re-created.

Tages (Tay'-ges): Etruscan god of divination and fortunetelling.

Thanatos: Greek god who is the personification of death, reminiscent of the Hunter, but with a sword rather than bow and arrow.

Thor: Norse god of thunder, storms, and weather.

Tunni: Finnish god of death and the Underworld.

Vulcan: God of fire and molten lava.

Yama: God of India who rules the land of the dead; he rides a black thunder horse, and thus relates to the Celtic Wild Hunt.

Goddesses

Aine: Celtic goddess of the Moon, crops, and cattle.

Angerona: Goddess of secret names.

Athena: Greek goddess of war and wisdom.

Badb: Celtic goddess of war; hag image of the Morrigan trinity.

Bellona: Goddess of war and battle skill.

Black Annis: Celtic hag goddess who collects the dead for the death passage.

Bone Mother: Slavic hag goddess who gathers and tends the dead.

Cailleach (Ca'[a sound of apple]-lee-ack): Celtic crone goddess.

Cerridwen (Cerr'-id-dwen): Celtic goddess of grain, associated with the wolf, the sow, the cat, and magic; called the white goddess.

Cybele: Goddess of wild beasts, untamed nature, and caverns.

Demeter (De-mee'-ter or Dem'-e-ter): Goddess of grain and the changing of the seasons; she turns into the crone of the barren earth while her daughter visits in Hades.

Diana (Artemis in Greece): Huntress; lady of the wild animals.

Durga: Great Goddess of India whose weapons became the symbols of the tarot and playing cards; the dark aspect of the Hindu Triple Goddesses, Durga-Uma-Parvati; wed to Shiva; also called Mother of the World.

Freya: Norse goddess of witchcraft, prophecy, shamanism, Nature, fertility, and the dead; associated with cats.

Hecate (Hec'-a-tay): Dark goddess of the moon, accompanied by hounds, she was honored at crossroads and cemeteries, and was associated with magic, wisdom (especially occult knowledge), and wealth; seen as a triple goddess in many ancient statues.

Hel: Norse crone goddess of death, ruler of the Underworld, from whom the modern word Hell is derived.

Hulda (Mother Hulda): Underworld goddess who controls the weather and bestows wealth on hard-working women.

Kali: Dark aspect of Mother Nature goddess of India; she is the passage from life through death to new life.

Kalma: Finnish hag goddess of death.

Kupala: Slavic goddess of magic, herbs, springs, and rivers.

Libitina: Goddess of funeral rites.

Louhi: Finnish dark goddess of magic.

Macha: War goddess, part of the Morrigan.

Medb: Third aspect of Morrigan war goddess triad.

Minerva: Etruscan goddess of war and wisdom.

Nemesis: Goddess of destiny and retribution.

Persephone (Per-se'-fa-nee): Daughter of Demeter and married to Hades; she ate pomegranate seeds while in the Underworld and thus each year has to spend time away from the upper earth, which is when the earth goes dormant because her mother grieves.

Prisni: Dark goddess of the Earth, representing fertility and giver of life in India.

Ran: Norse sea goddess and crone aspect for those lost at sea.

Rhea (Ree'-ah): Dark aspect of the Great Mother, unable to prevent her children from being devoured by her husband Cronos until she hid one and fed Cronos a stone. This child was raised to overthrow his father; hence, Rhea is a goddess of early deaths.

Teiltui (Tell'sha): Goddess of the primordial Earth.

Appendix C

A Few Thoughts on the Sforza Tarot Deck

With the modern copy of the Sforza deck, the Devil and Tower cards are replacement cards, but with depictions that accurately reflect Medieval themes of the wellspring, the fount of life (and fertility) and enlightenment. It was with the revival of the classics in the Renaissance that the previously self-critical eye turned outward once more to become enraptured by the beauty of Nature, the glory of classical art, literature, and the joy of life.

The Devil is not imprisoning people, but straddles a dry well to which a man and a woman have bound themselves. The cord that binds the man and woman is long and, while snug around her neck and his wrists, fits loosely through a ring at the base of the fount. The man's hands are tied at one end, yet it appears that the cord is simply wrapped twice around his wrists, then turned around itself a few twists to dangle next to his hands. The other end of the rope is slipknotted around the woman's neck, but her hands are free so that she can liberate herself or the man. Instead, she demonstrably rests her open right palm against the cracked fount. She gazes at the man, and he gazes at the Devil. All three figures are horned, but the man also has a tail (the Devil does not). The implication is different from the devil of Christian religion, displaying an acceptance of the situation by the people in bondage, something very real to people in a time of arranged political marriages and impenetrable social class differences.

The Tower card is amazingly uplifting to look at. The Tower is not struck by lightning, but is literally erupting with enlightenment, new opportunities, and hope for the future. Quite the opposite of a change coming from external forces, it is a change triggered by an internal force set free. The top of the Tower tears off, releasing both the Eclipsed Sun (symbolic of the Dark Lord and the only time the corona is visible) and the Star, while an older version of the hanged man and a young woman leap out with expressions of contentment and anticipation.

The Eclipsed Sun shows that the Light of Truth is best seen through darkness, which is the basic truth of divination—the Dark Aspect of the Divine lights the way for the Seeker.

Later tarot versions of the Tower card imply that life is ruled by the influence of powerful outside forces beyond one's control, but this is nowhere to be found in the Sforza Tower card. Instead, in the tone of Medieval mysticism, the power of enlightenment erupts from within, freeing truth and hope from isolation. These cards were condemned time and again by the Church because their deeper meaning can be seen with passing scrutiny—people enslave themselves and, contrary to the teaching of predestination, have the inner power to free themselves.

The high priestess in this deck is a Papess, which gives credence to the historical story of the woman who became "Pope" because she did not reveal she was a woman until being elected pope. She ruled only a very short time before being deposed, but "divine appointment" was in jeopardy. This card kept that knowledge alive and was no doubt a cause for consternation among the clergy. The Church leaders accused her of debaucheries, but the excuse seems a belated one intended to cover their shock at nearly losing their patriarchal dominance. The fear of electing a pagan to the Papacy was very real at the time, and their inadvertent election of a woman would have been cause for alarm.

A Few Thoughts on the Sforza Tarot Deck

The Fool card is easily recognizeable as the Fool of the Morris Dancers of England and their counterparts, still in evidence in modern Romania. As far-flung as these nations are, the Fool is a duplicate of the Sforza card, which depicts a man with a long cudgel and feathers stuck in his hair. In real life, he dances with the troupe that awakens the Earth at Springtime. He is the figure of fertility, creativity, and fearless productivity, for in the card it is his genitals that are nearly exposed, not his buttocks, and there is no dog nipping at his heels.

The Romanian tradition states that Fairy maidens taught a group of men to do a dance to bring prosperity to the farms. The men need to disguise themselves as women in order to perform this dance, but today they look nearly like the Morris Dancers of England. The style of dance involves foot work typical of the dances seen in Andalusia, Galicia, Ireland, and Scotland, and shows a connection with these Celtic traditions. The Romanian men dance in a circle and carry sticks to help balance themselves as they perform rapid staccato foot work accented by the ring of small bells strapped to their ankles. The group's fool also carries a stick, but he has the license to play Chaos with the dancers, teasing and trying to trip them up. Yet he, too, may be called on to demonstrate his expertise, so he needs to be among the best of the dancers. The troupe carries grain, the dark power herb of wormwood, and a decorated staff, as they make the rounds of all the farmsteads where they are warmly greeted. They dance, and then move on.

When they have visited all the farms, the dancers and Fool go to a hilltop where they bury the wormwood and grain. They lay down the staff and the dancers line up. Each dancer in turn presses down the mound with his feet and jumps over the staff. Now they are finished with their work and they remove their decorative hats, shake hands, and go to their homes.

The development of the ritual is lost in antiquity, but the meaning remembered is that the Earth is being awakened for the start of Spring so that bountiful crops will grow and prosperity will come for all in the coming year. This is a recurring theme in paganism, and attests to the resillience and widespread remembrance of the Old Religion of Nature.

The Moon card is the Goddess Diana with her silver bow, broken because she has accidentally killed the one she loved, but holding the Crone's Crescent Moon in her upraised hand, she is the Promise of life renewed. While at first glance the bow may appear to be a cord, the oddly stiff curves (and the use of a magnifying glass) reveal the cord to be a bow of twisted silver with smooth curved ends. It is bent sharply and only coincidentally near enough to a flounce of the goddess' dress to be mistaken for a cord. The cord of her dress is gold and ties above the same flounce. The picture shows that the Moon Goddess has the power of life through that passage called death—she is Crone, Maiden, and Mother all at once, and feared by the Church. This same Goddess may be seen in the card usually identified as the Star, and possibly again as Temperance. In the Star card, she wears a blue dress sprinkled with shooting stars, and a green-lined red mantle patterned with brilliant stars. In her upraised left hand a star rests in her open palm. Diana, called Artemis in Ephesus and later called the Goddess of the Witches, was a very popular goddess in the Roman Empire.

The hermit card is not that at all, but a well-dressed Father Time figure holding an encased hour glass in one hand as he leans upon a staff. He is the old year, the Holly King, wisdom and the Winter Solstice. His white beard and merry eyes bespeak the origins of St. Nicholas, not as a Christian bishop, but as Father Solstice, who is still called Father Christmas in Europe and Father Birth (Papa Natal) in Spanish language countries. He heralds the yearly birth of the Oak King, the Sun.

The Sforza card of the Chariot is not after the Egyptian or Roman style, but more similar to the four-wheeled wagon of the Celts or Etruscans. It is a high platform pulled by golden-winged, white horses controlled without reins, not by a charioteer, but by a stately woman who sits serenely upon a throne at the fore of the platform, crowned and holding an orb and scepter. Although only two wheels are visible, the platform disappears off the card, and its size and length make it necessarily at least four-wheeled. The image matches metal artifacts depicting Etruscan wagons with the rider atop the flatbed. The artistic approach is significantly different from the images used in the Chariot cards most often seen today, and the power here is decidedly feminine.

The Strength card shows not a woman and a lion, but Heracles (Roman Hercules) with his club and a lion. The typical pagan depiction of Heracles with a club in one hand and a lion's skin draped across the other arm comes to mind. The depiction of a woman and lion in modern decks may be an attempt to reclaim the role of feminine power implied in the earlier version of the Moon card and the Chariot card.

The Wheel of Fortune card contains a wry joke that bespeaks a truism even today. The person at the bottom of the wheel actually supports it, carrying the weight (or fortune) of others upon his back. One person ascends on one side, another sits regally on top, an orb in his hand, and a third descends headlong on the other side of the wheel. At the middle sits a blindfolded, winged woman with her hands outstretched, palms down at either side. She is Fata Morgana, the personification of Blind Fate, who neither judges nor intercedes.

The humor comes from the ass's ears on the youth ascending the wheel and on the one atop it. The one who descends and the old man beneath do not have the ears of an ass. The message is clear—Blind Luck allows young asses to rule on the backs of older and wiser men, and by the time they have ruled long enough to gain wisdom, they are deposed by young asses. This is a worldwide perception of the undeserving having and the deserving not, hence, blind luck.

The Magician card does not have the infinity symbol above the mage, but the man's floppy hat brim may have been mis-transcribed later to be an image of the sideways 8. He sits at a simple table and has a wand in one hand. On the table are a knife, a cup, two small round objects (nut shells perhaps) and what appears to be a hat of metal or a disk with a hub, possibly a scrying tool.

The Sun card shows a cherub rushing across the sky with the red sun in his upraised hands. The Sun is the face of Apollo, and the cherub wears a red-beaded necklace reminiscent of the necklace worn by the Goddess in her descent into the Underworld—hence, night has passed and the dawn comes.

The World card shows the influence of the Medieval Christian preoccupation with the idea of a heavenly New Jerusalem established on earth. In the card, the city is brought from heaven by two cheribum. The walled castle depicted, though, is a contemporary fifteenth century metaphor for a secure and complete city; a place that is self-sufficient and whole while all around there is warfare.

Death is represented as a skeletal Hunter with long bow and arrow. He stands with his eye sockets unwrapped, having an opened blindfold swirled around his head as if to say that through death is the unknown made known; or the previous arrow having been shot without discrimination, now is when the quarry is revealed to Death. The cloth should not be confused for a headbinding used to keep the jaw of a corpse shut. Such a binding went around the head vertically, passing under the chin and secured at the top of the head, but the cloth on Death is wrapped horizontally above the eyes so that if one visualizes the loose ends passing back across the eye sockets and tied at the back of the skull, the image is complete.

The card for Judgement is more like one of rebirth. It shows a bearded, god-like figure (patterned after classical statues of Zeus) with a sword in one hand and an orb in another, looking rather like the elderly gentleman from the hermit/father time card. Two angels sound trumpets and from a stone sarcophagus rise up three naked people—a young man, a young woman, and between them, an elderly, bearded man. This is reminiscent of the pagan reverence for ancestors and kinship.

Justice is a crowned woman holding an upright sword in one hand and scales in the other. She is not blindfolded, but on a hillside behind her is a knight wielding his sword as his steed carries him onward to engage an unseen foe. This is more than justice—this is the dark aspect of retribution, or justice achieved through the actions of a representative or an agent. In this deck, clearly Luck is blind, but Justice is intentional.

Some of the cards of modern decks, or the names applied to the cards, do not clearly reflect their intuitive meanings. In the case of Temperance, for example, the word means restraint and moderation rather than a balance or flow between two worlds or consciousnesses.

The Sforza card of Temperance appears to be Diana once more, arrayed in a blue gown with golden stars. She pours not water but dark wine—probably blackberry or elderberry wine, sacred to the Dark Lord and Dark Goddess respectively—from one pitcher into another. This is a practice that lets the wine breathe before being served, and again, she is the center of images relating to the life-cycle. In pagan tradition, adapted into Christianity, wine is the lifeblood of the God of Resurrection, Dionysus (or Jesus). The pagan perspective is revealed in this card, however, for it is the Goddess that controls this flow of life and gives it the breath of life.

The first twelve cards may be visualized in pagan pairs of either similarity or polarity: Greenman and Witch; High Priestess and High Priest; Mother Earth and Horned God; Lord and Lady of Greenwood and Wagon; Crone and Father Time; Wheel and Justice. The next six cards may be grouped as progressive pairs: Hanged Man and Tower; Fountain and Star; The Destroyer and Lord of Shadows. The last four cards of the major arcana represent the ultimate of the two sets of pairings. The first pairings of similarity/polarity are capped by the Moon and Sun, and the second pairings of progression are finalized by Harvest and the Universe.

The Greenman and the Witch are both Earth powers, with one being the power as exhibited by Nature and the other being the one who connects with and utilizes the powers of Nature. The High Priestess and High Priest are two approaches to Divine Empowerment. Mother Earth and the Horned God are complimentary emblems of fertility and the ability to both create and tend what is created.

The Greenwood and Wagon cards both represent a balance, but the methods are different. The Crone and Father Time are images of wisdom and the power gained through life experience and education. The Wheel and Justice relate to both unjust and just rewards, for it is in these two cards that gains for both the undeserving and the deserving are reflected and recognized. The Wheel and Justice cards address a point that creates a quandary in mainstream religion—namely that *bad* things do happen to *good* people, and *good* things do happen to *bad* people. These cards also reflect that matters are on an upswing to improvement, or that balance can be regained, even by retribution.

From here, the cards become sequential pairs. The Hanged Man and the Tower show movement from meditative inaction to sudden enlightenment with subsequent change resulting. The Fountain and the Star relate to each other through being inspired, yet remaining grounded. The first shows the rational and intuitive in lively harmony, while the the second shows that inspiration can be manifested.

The Destroyer and Lord of Shadows are two images of the Underworld. The first card reflects a condition wrought by personal decision that may be changed simply by having the will to do so. There are times when willing bondage has its place in the mind of the person so bonded, such as when a dissatisfied couple remain together for the sake of the children. By recognizing this as an agreement to benefit others, anger and emotional disharmony can be dealt with in a more rational manner. This card could relate to not wanting to take a chance at finding a new job, and staying with one that may have little more than monetary compensation. The Lord of Shadows is sequential in that there is a transition from bondage to freedom through a change that creates a new life. In either case, He is not judgmental, but compassionate and understanding.

The Moon and the Sun are generally seen as intuitive and rational polarities—Goddess and God symbols—but these two bodies are similar in that they greatly affect life on earth. The waters and the land; nourishment and growth; tandem influences that are both needed for a fruitful earth-life. The one lights the night while the other lights the day, and both have their times of greater or lesser light through lunar phases, the Solstices, and eclipses, so that it is up to individuals to keep these lights in their hearts.

With the Moon, particularly in reverse, there are times when responsibilities and duty interfere with one's sense of connection with the whole of existence. This is not necessarily a bad thing, because the reality is that mundane matters need attention—the laundry has to be done, the meals prepared, the car tuned, the tires rotated, the lawn mowed, the children attended to and so forth. So there will be times when the Moon may feel reversed in one's life simply because there is not a lot of time for introspection and subconscious connecting. Being aware of this may help one to reorganize one's time to create a more balanced life.

The Harvest and Universe cards demonstrate that good choices have been made and progress toward unity with the Universe has been achieved. These are the easiest cards to read and perhaps the hardest to understand because they may appear to mean that everything is ended satisfactorily—the great "ta-da" of life, take a bow, exit stage left, but these cards relate to a particular aspect or a level of development in one's life. As long as a person is reading cards, there is never a finality, merely an ending that leads to a new or renewed beginning, or a realignment of one's focus into another area of personal, spiritual, or emotional development. The more these cards seem to conclude a matter, the more they point to new horizons.

The tarot can be used for both self development and divination, and the major arcana are guiding influences for both. While it is possible to commit the minor arcana to memory, the type of deck used could make this difficult. Each deck has its own personality and style, so that the reading for the four of cups, as an example, may vary, depending upon the depiction. In some decks it may visually infer satiation, in another a storing up of inspiration, and in yet others having used stored inspiration and being ready to take on a new challenge or opportunity coming into play. By using a deck with no images for the four suits of ace to ten, the reader may want to pick a general formula for each card and let intuitive insight frame the meaning by what lies around it.

The upright and reversed meanings of the minor arcana may be used with a deck depicting scenes on each card, but for a deck which uses only arrangements of implements like the Sforza, (wands, swords, cups, and disks) numbering from 1 to 10, the upright or reversed meanings are derived by the surrounding cards. The aspect of a card may be favorable or unfavorable depending on its position in the spread or on the cards around it. The Court Cards are King, Queen, Knight (or Prince), and Page (or Princess), and these may refer to individuals or to circumstances depending upon their aspect. As with all divination, feelings, visions, and intuition play an important role in recognizing the aspect, and thus the meaning, of a card.

When a reader has used a deck a number of times, the cards fall appropriately for the deck being used, so that overall the intuitive link with the Dark Goddess and Dark God will come into focus, no matter what system the reader develops, as long as the connection between reader and Dark Lady/Dark Lord is there.

Any tarot deck may be reinterpreted with a dark focus for the upright and reversed cards, which represents the basic (Green) foundational level of Witchcraft.

All divinations drawing upon the intuitive and psychic powers of the reader to interpret the throw of the cards are Moon-sided. Since it is the wisdom and knowledge of the unknown that is sought in divination, this draws upon the dark aspect of the goddess, the Crone. It is she who gives intuitive insights to those who understand her means of communication. When using divination, one taps into intuitive perceptions that are an unleashing of the subconscious mind to flow with the Universal Mind. This is a dark-sided practice, and is a way for people to actively take part in the entirety of existence. Light and dark in balance are needed for both a whole Universe and a whole individual. There must be a recognition that dark is not synonymous with evil, but with intuitive perception and non-conscious awareness—an altered state of awareness that can be triggered by releasing the subconscious mind from its bonds of conscious vision.

This is where the meaning of terms comes back in relation to the usage of the word game. To say that the tarrochi was a game is to not recognize that the actions of the Divine (particularly in the religious concepts of the people of India who invented the cards) are seen as play. Life is a game, then, and when living becomes playing, freedom is achieved. To play, the dark aspect of the mind has to be embraced, not as a thing of fears, but as a thing that is different—as Other.

When one can slip into the altered state, one becomes Other. The individual becomes Sidhe. This word for the Elves is also the

Sanskrit word for being charged with energy, and hints at a connection between the two. This state of being energized is not a permanent state, and thus one's Self as Sidhe slips back into Otherworld where the Sidhe self can find repose and refreshment. To communicate with Otherworld is to confront Truth without artifice—thus divination is a path to Truth, and the Light of Truth resides unrestrained in the Dark.

People who try to retain the Sidhe Self for extended periods of time wear out their physical form. They display symptoms of restlessness, coupled with the inability to take action in the conscious plane. This can be mistaken for depression, but it is actually fatigue of the nervous system from over-extended contact with the dark aspect. As ever, a balance must be maintained. Just as existence is not all light, it is not all dark. Trying to live solely in either aspect will generate behaviorial problems, everything from the transitory intoxication of religious revivalism to the lingering malaise of morose dissatisfaction. The former requires constant "hits" of religious frenzy, while the latter drains a person into an inability to function.

When a person has been very involved in connectedness with the dark aspect and finds it difficult to release the contact—it is after all a union with the Wisdom of the Universe—for the sake of physical health, a deliberate effort must be undertaken to restore the Balance within. This can be accomplished through a releasing ritual that involves lighting a white votive candle and grounding the excess energy. The candle provides a point of focus and the white color evokes a feeling of peace, pureness, and wholeness.

Sit comfortably on the floor (or ground if done out-of-doors) and place both palms flat on the floor. Visualize the excessive, sparking energy as collecting into a pool centered above the eyes and then drain that pool down the arms, out of the palms, into the floor, and through to the earth beneath. When this is done, expel the air in the lungs, take a deep breath, expel it, repeat, and resume normal breathing. Snuff out the candle to physically center on the ending of the psychic connection for now, and take some refreshment. Now it is time to resume the conscious part of life.

With experience, a person soon learns the level of tolerance for the connection with the Dark Lady and Dark Lord that one's body can handle. Through respecting one's own limitations and taking progressive steps in making contact, those boundaries can be expanded to the point where one can live virtually in both worlds at once. Such people have a very balanced outlook on life and death, and their Universe is extended as it suits them. Divination with the tarot is a very good way to learn the language of the intuitive mind and connect with the Goddess of the Dark Moon and the Lord of Shadows.

Appendix D

Mail Order Supplies

Abyss Distribution
48 Chester Road
Chester, MA 01011–9735
(413) 623–2155
email: AbyssDist@aol.com

Eye of the Cat
3314 E. Broadway
Long Beach, CA 90803
(310) 438–3569

Eye of the Day
P.O. Box 21261
Boulder, CO 80308
1–800–717–3307

JBL Statues
P.O. Box 163
Crozet, VA 22932
(World Wide Web site) http://www.jblstatue.com/

LUNATRIX
P.O. Box 800482
Santa Clarita, CA 91380–0482

MAGIC BOOK STORE
2306 Highland Avenue
National City, CA 91950
(619) 477–5260

ROOTS AND WINGS
16607 Barberry , C2
Southgate, MI 48195
(313) 285–3679

WHITE LIGHT PENTACLES/SACRED SPIRIT PRODUCTS
P.O. Box 8163
Salem, MA 01971–8163

WORLDWIDE CURIO HOUSE
P.O. Box 17095
Minneapolis, MN 55417

Non-Mail Order Sales

DRAGONWOOD catalog on Internet sales at
www.dragonwood.com

HERNE'S HOLLOW
1211 Hillcrest Street
Orlando, FL 32803
(407) 895–7439.

Appendix E

Black Mirrors and Ogham Sticks

It is generally easy to find a black mirror or set of ogham fews these days—nearly any New Age shop or catalog carries them, as do most of the resources listed in Appendix D. Should you want to make your own, however, here are simple methods for both items.

Make Your Own Black Mirror

A mirror is really only a piece of glass with one side coated or painted to keep light rays from passing through. The light is then reflected back to the viewer. Take a piece of circular glass and wash it with spring water. Dry it and let it sit in the moonlight during a full moon and then during a dark moon. Next, paint the back of the glass with black enamel and let it dry. Cut out a piece of black felt to fit the back of the mirror and glue it into place. Another method of construction is to paint a circle of black enamel in the center of a circle of silver aluminum foil. While the paint is still tacky, but n⁄ wet, add a clear glue to the foil rim. Lay the painted foil against⁄ clean glass and carefully press it onto the glass. This leaves a ck edge around the mirror. After this dries, you can then glue t⁄ foil felt to the back of the mirror to avoid scratching or scrapi⁄ and paint.

Use the tool dedication ritual to energize your mirror. You may want to set the mirror in a decorative frame or set it on a holder such as used to display plates. Keep it covered with a black cloth when not in use. To retain the focus of the energies, only use the mirror in your magical workings. Imbolc is a good time to cleanse and re-dedicate all your tools, including this one.

Make Your Own Ogham Fews

Ogham sticks or fews are another simple tool to create for yourself. Hardware and home supply shops tend to carry a nice selection of wood strips for various edgings. You can get a length of thin wood stripping that is plain, or decorated (as with a variety of leaves). Measure the strip and mark so you may cut the wood for even lengths of fews—1 to 1½ inches per few should suffice. On the wood, incise an ogham symbol in each marked-off section. Since these are merely lines, it is an easy bit of woodcarving! Cut the strips to free the individual fews. You may want to stain the symbols or paint the whole with a clear varnish.

Use the tool dedication ritual to consecrate your fews, and then store them in a dark pouch or bag. The casting cloth, already described, may be folded and placed inside the bag with the fews or may be the container for the fews when gathered and tied with the fews inside.

Selected Bibliography

Aoumiel (Ann Moura). *Dancing Shadows: The Roots of Western Religious Beliefs*. St. Paul: Llewellyn Publications, 1994.

Baring, Anne and Jules Cashford. *The Myth of the Goddess*. London: Arkana, Penguin Books, 1993.

Briggs, Katherine. *An Encyclopedia of Fairies, Hobgoblins, Brownies, Bogies, and Other Supernatural Creatures*. New York: Pantheon Books, 1976.

Buckland, Raymond. *Buckland's Complete Book of Witchcraft*. St. Paul: Llewellyn Publications, 1993.

Campbell, Joseph. *The Masks of God: Oriental Mythology*. New York: Penguin Books, 1976.

———. *The Masks of God: Primitive Mythology*. New York: Penguin Books, 1976.

Carylon, Richard. *A Guide to the Gods*. New York: Quill, William Morrow, 1981.

Cavendish, Richard. *The Black Arts*. New York: Perigee Books, The Berkeley Publishing Group, 1967.

Conway, D. J. *Celtic Magic*. St. Paul: Llewellyn Publications, 1990.

Cunliffe, Barry. *The Celtic World*. New York: Greenwich House, Crown Publishers, Inc., 1986.

Selected Bibliography

Cunningham, Scott. *The Complete Book of Incense, Oils & Brews*. St. Paul: Llewellyn Publications, 1990.

Durant, Will. *The Story of Civilization: Our Oriental Heritage* (Volume I). New York: Simon & Schuster, 1954.

——. *The Story of Civilization: The Life of Greece* (Volume II). New York: Simon & Schuster, 1966.

——. *The Story of Civilization: The Age of Faith* (Volume IV). New York: Simon & Schuster, 1950.

Eliot, Alexander. *The Universal Myths: Heroes, Gods, Tricksters and Others*. New York: Meridian Books, 1990.

Evans-Wentz, W. Y. *The Fairy-Faith in Celtic Countries*. New York: Carol Publishing Group, 1994.

Francisis, Alphonso de. *Pompeii*. Napoli, Italy: Interdipress, 1972.

Gimbutas, Marija. *The Civilization of the Goddess: The World of Old Europe*. Edited by Joan Marler. San Francisco: HarperCollins Publishers, 1991.

González-Wippler, Migene. *The Complete Book of Spells, Ceremonies & Magic*. St. Paul: Llewellyn Publications, 1988.

Goodrich, Norma Lorre. *Priestesses*. New York: Harper Perennial, 1989.

Graves, Robert. *The White Goddess: A Historical Grammar of Poetic Myth*. New York: The Noonday Press, Farrar, Straus and Giroux, amended and enlarged edition, 1966.

Green, Marian. *A Witch Alone*. London: The Aquarian Press, 1991.

Kramker, S. N. *The Sumerians: Their History, Culture, and Character*. Chicago: The University of Chicago Press, 1963.

Llewellyn's *1998 Magical Almanac*. St. Paul: Llewellyn Publications, 1997.

Massa, Aldo. *The World of the Etruscans*. Translated by John Christmas. Geneve, Italy: Minerva, 1989.

Moura, Ann. *Green Witchcraft: Folk Magic, Fairy Lore & Herb Craft*. St. Paul: Llewellyn Publications, 1996.

Pepper, Wilcox, et al. *The Witches' Almanac.* Cambridge: Pentacle Press, 1992–93, 1993–94.

Scholem, Gershom. *Origins of the Kabbalah.* English translation by The Jewish Publication Society, 1987. Berlin: Walter de Gruyer & Co., 1962. Third printing, Princeton: University of Princeton, 1990.

Scott, Michael. *Irish Folk and Fairy Tale Omnibus.* UK: Sphere Books Ltd., 1983; New York: Barnes & Noble Books, 1983.

Sjoo, Monica and Barbara Mor. *The Great Cosmic Mother.* San Francisco: HarperCollins Publishers, 1991.

Squire, Charles. *Celtic Myth and Legend.* Newcastle: Newcastle Publishing Co., Inc., 1975.

Stone, Merlin. *When God Was a Woman.* New York: Dorset Press, 1976.

Taylour, Lord William. *The Mycenaneans.* London: Thames and Hudson Ltd., 1994.

Thorsson, Edred. *The Book of Ogham: The Celtic Tree Oracle.* St. Paul: Llewellyn Publications, 1992.

——. *Northern Magic: Mysteries of the Norse, Germans & English.* St. Paul: Llewellyn Publications, 1992.

Walker, Barbara. *The Crone: Woman of Age Wisdom and Power.* San Francisco: HarperCollins Publishers, 1985.

Woolley, C. Leonard. *The Sumerians.* New York: W. W. Norton & Company, 1965.

Index

Index

☽ REACH FOR THE MOON

Llewellyn publishes hundreds of books on your favorite subjects! To get these exciting books, including the ones on the following pages, check your local bookstore or order them directly from Llewellyn.

ORDER BY PHONE
- Call toll-free within the U.S. and Canada, 1-800-THE MOON
- In Minnesota, call (612) 291-1970
- We accept VISA, MasterCard, and American Express

ORDER BY MAIL
- Send the full price of your order (MN residents add 7% sales tax) in U.S. funds, plus postage & handling to:

  Llewellyn Worldwide
  P.O. Box 64383, Dept. K689-0
  St. Paul, MN 55164–0383, U.S.A.

POSTAGE & HANDLING
(For the U.S., Canada, and Mexico)
- $4.00 for orders $15.00 and under
- $5.00 for orders over $15.00
- No charge for orders over $100.00

We ship UPS in the continental United States. We ship standard mail to P.O. boxes. Orders shipped to Alaska, Hawaii, The Virgin Islands, and Puerto Rico are sent first-class mail. Orders shipped to Canada and Mexico are sent surface mail.

International orders: Airmail—add freight equal to price of each book to the total price of order, plus $5.00 for each non-book item (audio tapes, etc.).

Surface mail—Add $1.00 per item.

Allow 2 weeks for delivery on all orders.
Postage and handling rates subject to change.

DISCOUNTS
We offer a 20% discount to group leaders or agents. You must order a minimum of 5 copies of the same book to get our special quantity price.

FREE CATALOG

Get a free copy of our color catalog, *New Worlds of Mind and Spirit*. Subscribe for just $10.00 in the United States and Canada ($30.00 overseas, airmail). Many bookstores carry *New Worlds*—ask for it!

Visit our web site at www.llewellyn.com for more information.

GREEN WITCHCRAFT
Folk Magic, Fairy Lore & Herb Craft

Ann Moura

1-56718-690-4
6 x 9, 288 pp.
illustrated
$14.95

Very little has been written about traditional family practices of the Old Religion simply because such information has not been offered for popular consumption. If you have no contacts with these traditions, *Green Witchcraft* will meet your need for a practice based in family and natural Witchcraft traditions.

Green Witchcraft describes the worship of nature and the use of herbs that have been part of human culture from the earliest times. It relates to the Lord & Lady of Greenwood, the Primal Father and Mother, and to the Earth Spirits called Faeries.

Green Witchcraft traces the historic and folk background of this path and teaches its practical techniques. Learn the basics of Witchcraft from a third-generation, traditional family Green Witch who openly shares from her own experiences. Through a how-to format you'll learn rites of passage, activities for Sabbats and Esbats, Fairy lore, self-dedication, self-initiation, spellwork, herbcraft and divination.

This practical handbook is an invitation to explore, identify and adapt the Green elements of Witchcraft that work for you, today.

You are a blend of balancing energies: masculine and feminine, active and passive, and light and dark. However, most books on spirituality and empowerment avoid addressing your psyche's native darker aspects—even though it's vital that you claim your "darkness" to becoming a whole, integrated, empowered person.

Dark Moon Mysteries is the first book to explore the "dark side" of spirit, ritual, symbol, psyche, and magic. It is also the first book on Witchcraft to make use of storytelling to access wisdom and in-sight, in the tradition of Women Who Run with the Wolves. This book weaves together Jungian analysis, the practical application of imagery from ancient fairy tales, and contemporary Witchcraft to help you come to grips with the darker shades of your being. You'll use magic, rituals, dance, guided journeys, and more to explore your deep consciousness.

Work spiritually and magically with the Dark Moon to touch upon the very source of your inner power and to move beyond your fears and limitations. Embrace all aspects of your psyche and follow the true path of the Witch, shaman, magician and mystic.

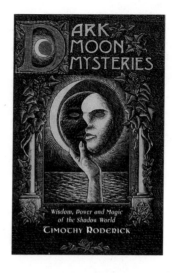

DARK MOON MYSTERIES
Wisdom, Power and Magick of the Shadow World

Timothy Roderick

1-56718-345-X
240 pp., 6 x 9
softcover
$14.95

**LORD OF
LIGHT
& SHADOW**
The Many Faces
of the God

D. J. Conway

1-56178-177-5
240 pp., 6 x 9
illus., softcover
$14.95

Early humans revered the great Goddess and all Her personalized aspects, but they also revered the God as Her necessary and important consort/lover/son. Lord of Light and Shadow leads you through the myths of the world's diverse cultures to find the archetypal Pagan God hidden behind all of them. He is a being with the traits and aspects that women secretly desire in men, and that men desire to emulate. The patriarchal religions assimilated the ancient spirit of the Pagan God—in one form or another—into their scriptures. Yet, despite the deliberate changes to his identity, there is something about the God that could never be destroyed. By searching for the original Pagan God in these mythologies, you will find his spiritual essence and the path to the truth.

Enjoy the first book written for Pagan parents! The number of Witches raising children to the Craft is growing. The need for mutual support is rising—yet until now, there have been no books that speak to a Wiccan family's needs and experience. Finally, here is *The Family Wicca Book*, full to the brim with rituals, projects, encouragement and practical discussion of real-life challenges. You'll find lots of ideas to use right away.

Is magic safe for children? Why do some people think Wiccans are Satanists? How do you make friends with spirits and little people in the local woods? Find out how one Wiccan family gives clear and honest answers to questions that in-trigue pagans all over the world.

When you want to ground your family in Wicca without ugly "bashing;" explain life, sex, and death without embarrassment; and add to your Sabbats without much trouble or expense, *The Family Wicca Book* is required reading. You'll refer to it again and again as your traditions grow with your family.

THE FAMILY WICCA BOOK
The Craft for Parents & Children

Ashleen O'Gaea

0-87542-591-7
240 pgs., 5 ¼ x 8
illus., softcover
$9.95

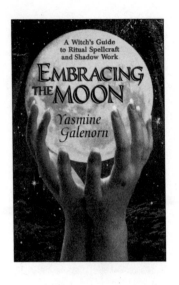

EMBRACING THE MOON
A Witch's Guide to Rituals, Spellcraft & Shadow Work

Yasmine Galenorn

1-56718-304-2
6 x 9, 312 pp.
illustrated
$14.95

Do you feel like toasting the Gods with a glass of mead as you revel in the joys of life? Ever wish you could creep through the mists at night, hunting the Wild Lord? *Embracing the Moon* takes you into the core of Witchcraft, helping you weave magic into your daily routine. The spells and rituals are designed to give you the flexibility to experiment so that you are not locked into dogmatic, rigid degree-systems. Written to encompass both beginning and advanced practitioners, *Embracing the Moon* explores the mystical side of natural magic while keeping a common-sense attitude.

Packed not only with spells and rituals, but recipes for oils, spell powders and charms, this book is based on personal experience; the author dots the pages with her own stories and anecdotes to give you fascinating, and sometimes humorous, examples of what you might expect out of working with her system of magic.

Wicca is a book of life, and how to live magically, spiritually, and wholly attuned with Nature. It is a book of sense and common sense, not only about Magick, but about religion and one of the most critical issues of today: how to achieve the much needed and wholesome relationship with our Earth. Cunningham presents Wicca as it is today: a gentle, Earth-oriented religion dedicated to the Goddess and God. This book fulfills a need for a practical guide to solitary Wicca—a need which no previous book has fulfilled.

Here is a positive, practical introduction to the religion of Wicca, designed so that any interested person can learn to practice the religion alone, anywhere in the world. It presents Wicca honestly and clearly, without the pseudo-history that permeates other books. It shows that Wicca is a vital, satisfying part of twentieth century life.

This book presents the theory and practice of Wicca from an individual's perspective. The section on the Standing Stones Book of Shadows contains solitary rituals for the Esbats and Sabbats. This book, based on the author's nearly two decades of Wiccan practice, presents an eclectic picture of various aspects of this religion. Exercises designed to develop magical proficiency, a self-dedication ritual, herb, crystal and rune magic, as well as recipes for Sabbat feasts, are included in this excellent book.

WICCA
A Guide for the Solitary Practitioner

Scott Cunningham

0-87542-118-0
240 pp., 6 x 9
illus., softcover
$9.95

To Order, Call 1–800–THE–MOON
Prices subject to change without notice.

LIVING WICCA
A Further Guide
for the
Solitary Practitioner

Scott Cunningham

0-87542-184-9
208 pp., 6 x 9
illus., softcover
$12.95

Living Wicca is the long-awaited sequel to Scott Cunningham's successful *Wicca: a Guide for the Solitary Practitioner.* This book is for those who have made the conscious decision to bring their Wiccan spirituality into their everyday lives. It provides solitary practitioners with the tools and added insights that will enable them to blaze their own spiritual paths—to become their own high priests and priestesses.

Living Wicca takes a philosophical look at the questions, practices, and differences within Witchcraft. It covers the various tools of learning available to the practitioner, the importance of secrecy in one's practice, guidelines to performing ritual when ill, magical names, initiation, and the Mysteries. It discusses the benefits of daily prayer and meditation, making offerings to the gods, how to develop a prayerful attitude, and how to perform Wiccan rites when away from home or in emergency situations.

Unlike any other book on the subject, *Living Wicca* is a step-by-step guide to creating your own Wiccan tradition and personal vision of the gods, designing your personal ritual and symbols, developing your own book of shadows, and truly living your Craft.